PRAISE FOR *HOW'S YOUR SOUL?*

"I have been blessed to have Judah not only as my pastor but as my friend. When I see Judah preach, or read what he writes, it is experiencing someone doing exactly what they were created to do."

—Tim Tebow, speaker, activist, bestselling author

"Without question, one of the greatest communicators of our generation is Judah Smith. His ability to captivate a crowd is only surpassed by his care and concern for the individual. I have proudly watched as his leadership capacity has grown and stretched amidst all the seasons of life—including grief, heartache, and change. Regardless of what season you are in, there is no one I could think of more qualified and enjoyable to sit down with and answer the question 'How's your soul?' Enjoy finding humor, wisdom, and godly counsel within these pages."

—Brian Houston, founder and global
senior pastor, Hillsong Church

"Judah Smith has spent his life doing 'soul work.' In *How's Your Soul?*, he shares his guidance for gaining a better understanding of what's going on inside each and every one of us. Soul work is life work."

—Maria Shriver, journalist, producer,
and bestselling author

"Judah Smith is an exceptional writer and communicator. His ability to tell a story and at the same time make a life-changing point is second to none. In *How's Your Soul?*, he is honest with his own journey, and at the same time encourages all of us to get to that place called home—that sense of peace even within the fast-paced world in which we live. You will laugh, learn, and be given practical tools as you make the journey to a healthy soul. Get this book, and get one for a friend!"

—Holly Wagner, pastor, Oasis Church
LA; author, *Find Your Brave*

HOW'S YOUR SOUL?

HOW'S YOUR SOUL?

WHY EVERYTHING YOU WANT IN LIFE
STARTS WITH THE INSIDE YOU

JUDAH SMITH

NELSON
BOOKS

An Imprint of Thomas Nelson

Published in Nashville, Tennessee, by Nelson Books, an imprint of Thomas Nelson. Nelson Books and Thomas Nelson are registered trademarks of HarperCollins Christian Publishing, Inc.

Published in association with the literary agency of The FEDD Agency, Inc., Post Office Box 341973, Austin, Texas 78734.

Thomas Nelson titles may be purchased in bulk for educational, business, fundraising, or sales promotional use. For information, please e-mail SpecialMarkets@ ThomasNelson.com.

Unless otherwise noted, Scripture quotations are taken from the ESV˙ Bible (The Holy Bible, English Standard Version˙), copyright © 2001 by Crossway, a publishing ministry of Good News Publishers. Used by permission. All rights reserved.

Scripture quotations marked THE MESSAGE are from *The Message*. Copyright © by Eugene H. Peterson 1993, 1994, 1995, 1996, 2000, 2001, 2002. Used by permission of Tyndale House Publishers, Inc.

Scripture quotations marked NIV are taken from the Holy Bible, New International Version˙, NIV˙. Copyright © 1973, 1978, 1984, 2011 by Biblica, Inc.˙ Used by permission of Zondervan. All rights reserved worldwide. www.zondervan.com. The "NIV"and "New International Version" are trademarks registered in the United States Patent and Trademark Office by Biblica, Inc.˙

Scripture quotations marked NLT are from the Holy Bible, New Living Translation. © 1996, 2004, 2007, 2013 by Tyndale House Foundation. Used by permission of Tyndale House Publishers, Inc., Carol Stream, Illinois 60188. All rights reserved.

ISBN: 9780718039332 (eBook)
ISBN: 9780718096557 (signed)
ISBN: 9780718088606 (IE)

Library of Congress Cataloging-in-Publication Data

Names: Smith, Judah, author.
Title: How's your soul? : why everything you want in life starts with the inside you / Judah Smith.
Description: Nashville : Thomas Nelson, 2016. | Includes bibliographical references.
Identifiers: LCCN 2016014082 | ISBN 9780718039172
Subjects: LCSH: Contentment--Religious aspects--Christianity. |
  Desire--Religious aspects--Christianity. | Christianity--Psychology. | Soul.
Classification: LCC BV4647.C7 S55 2016 | DDC 248.4--dc23
LC record available at https://lccn.loc.gov/2016014082

Printed in the United States of America

16 17 18 19 20 RRD 6 5 4 3 2 1

To my sister Wendy, whom I admire,
look up to, and still want to be like

CONTENTS

Introduction   xi

ONE: HOME SWEET HOME   1

TWO: ORIGINAL HOME   17

THREE: SURPRISED BY MY SOUL   39

FOUR: AN ANCHOR FOR MY SOUL   61

FIVE: IS LOVE GOD OR IS GOD LOVE?   79

SIX: A QUIET SOUL   99

SEVEN: AN EFFECTIVE LIFE   119

EIGHT: NEW YOU   135

NINE: INSIDE JOB   155

TEN: HEAVEN   173

CONCLUSION   189

Acknowledgments   191

Notes   193

About the Author   195

INTRODUCTION

Have you ever had someone look you deep in the soul and ask, "Are you okay?"

I'm not talking about a casual acquaintance. I mean someone who really knows you. Someone who gets you. Someone who somehow picks up on your unspoken struggles and who cares enough to push and probe past your superficial "Yeah, I'm fine."

The fact the person has to ask if you are okay means you are probably *not* okay. Both of you know that. But the offer to dialogue about it is somehow comforting. Even healing.

"Actually . . . no. I don't think I am okay. I mean, I will be okay—I'm pretty sure, anyway. I'll get through this. But right now my world is upside down. I don't understand what I'm thinking or feeling."

"I'm here for you. If you want to talk, just let me know."

To be honest, there aren't too many friends like that out there. And even when people do try to dig deeper, we tend to avoid their soul-searching questions for as long as we can. Vulnerability is scary. It feels safer to be superficial.

"Me? Yeah, I'm great. My job is going well . . . I'm reaching my financial goals . . . I just signed with a recording studio . . . The kids are getting good grades . . . I'm hitting the gym regularly . . . yes, I'm good. Just tired, you know. No big deal. Why do you ask?"

We tend to use outward indicators of success to prove how "okay" we are. But none of these things—not wealth, not fame, not family, not goals reached—mean we are healthy and happy on the inside.

This is a book about being okay on the inside. It's a book about being satisfied, stable, and healthy on a soul level.

The "Are you okay?" question is scary, because it has to do with the real you—not with your achievements or activities, but with your emotions, your thoughts, your decisions, your values, and your desires.

For me personally, I often don't want to know the answer. Deep inside, I'm afraid I'm *not* okay. I have internal contradictions I would rather not face.

That is why this is probably the scariest book I've written to date. I know that is an odd thing for an author to admit, but it's true. Writing about inner health, emotional stability, and other soul-related topics is a vulnerable business, because before I am a writer or pastor or speaker, I am a human. How can I speak and teach on the subject when my own soul is bent and flawed?

This book is the result of wrestling with questions like these in my own life and experience. I am on a journey, just like everyone else. I'm not here to tell you what to believe or how to act. Yes, I've learned a few things along the way, and I hope they help you. But by no means am I an expert on the inside you.

I don't mean to imply that I am the final word on what a soul should look like or how to fix a broken heart.

When it comes to the human soul, I don't think any of us can claim to have everything figured out. More than twenty-five hundred years ago the prophet Jeremiah gave the ancient nation of Israel a message from God: "The heart is deceitful above all things, and desperately sick; who can understand it?" (17:9).

That's hardly encouraging. But Jeremiah wasn't being cynical—he was being honest. He was simply stating the human condition. He had apparently come face-to-face with the same fears we confront: that maybe deep inside we don't have it all together; maybe our insides are not okay.

God's message in Jeremiah doesn't stop there, though. The next verse says, "I the LORD search the heart and test the mind" (17:10). In other words, we can't always figure ourselves out, but God can. He knows us better than we know ourselves. That is why the heart of this book is not to elevate our human opinions or experiences, but to learn from the one who designed our souls in the first place: God.

You'll realize soon—if you don't know already—that I am a Bible guy and a Jesus guy. I believe God is real and he cares about what happens on this planet. I believe that the only way to make sense out of this life is to include God in our plans and equations.

Even if you aren't sure what you believe about God, or about Jesus, or about the Bible, I think a lot of what Scripture says will resonate with you. It is, after all, a collection of the wisdom and life experiences of some forty different authors written over nearly fifteen hundred years. So at the very least, I invite you to approach the Bible as a compendium of ancient wisdom and philosophy. Maybe there are some things you can glean from it that apply to your twenty-first-century life. And if the Bible is truly God's perfect, inspired message to mankind—as I believe it is—then it's worth hearing what the Creator has to say about this complicated thing we call the soul.

Why is this important? Why do our souls matter? Why should we care about the health of our souls? Because no matter who we are and no matter how long or how well we've been navigating life, there will be times when our souls find themselves in dark places—times when we doubt our internal stability and when we wonder if we are really okay.

In moments like those, how do we respond? Do we wait until we are perfect before proceeding? Do we search for six foolproof steps to soul stability? Do we freeze up in fear of failure?

Ultimately the stability and security and outcome of our souls need to be in the hands of someone who is bigger than our souls and greater than our turmoil. That someone is God, and he invites us to go on a journey of soul discovery and soul health with him.

one

HOME SWEET HOME

I despise traveling.

To be clear, I love *arriving*. Who doesn't like arriving? Arriving is exciting and exhilarating and sexy. But unfortunately you can't arrive without traveling. And traveling—the process of getting from point A to point B—can be a bit painful, particularly if it involves any form of mass transit. And by *mass transit* I mean traveling in herds with other humans.

Now, I have nothing against people. I love people. I'm a pastor, after all. But there is something about being sealed in a metal cylinder in the sky for hours on end with hundreds of strangers that is just . . . challenging. And claustrophobic. And maybe slightly terrifying.

That's why when I fly, I often pull a hoodie over my head and shut out the world. And it's also why, after any long trip, a peculiar emotion floods my being when I walk into my house.

It's the feeling of being *home*.

There's No Place Like Home, say doormats everywhere. *Welcome Home. Home, Sweet Home. Home Is Where the Heart Is. Home Is Where You Hang Your Hat. Your Home Is Your Castle.*

You get the idea.

There is no sensation on the planet quite like coming home. I'm sure you've felt it too. Your home may not be exquisite, it may not be extraordinary, it may not be extensive—but it's yours. Whether you own it, rent it, built it, or borrowed it, it's your home. Even if you have roommates and you all share a house, that one bedroom is your space. Your home is your sanity and your sanctuary. It is where you are fully yourself.

Home is therapeutic. I love coming home.

In particular, I love coming home to my own bathroom and my own toilet. That might be too honest, but we might as well start this book off right.

After being on the road for days and dealing with assorted public restrooms and hotel rooms, I will literally smile at my toilet. "Hey there, little buddy. Nice to see you. I've missed you."

You know the best part about using your own toilet? No seat covers needed. Is there anything more tedious, ridiculous, and inhumane than being in a public restroom and trying to figure out how to punch out the middle of those seat covers without sending the whole thing down the drain? I realize that in relation to the grand scale of the cosmos, and in light of the human plight and world peace and global warming, this is probably a petty problem. But in the moment, it's real.

At home, though, your toilet is clean, sanitary, and inviting—unless you have children who are potty training, in which case I actually recommend seat covers. And disinfectant. And hazmat suits. Or just give up and use public restrooms, because they will probably be cleaner.

Besides friendly bathrooms, here's something else I like about coming home: *drop spots.* As in, spots where you drop stuff. These are specific locations where you deposit whatever you are carrying the second you walk in the door.

Drop spots are one of the more underrated elements of home, but we all have them. Usually these drop spots are not planned. They evolve. Right *here* is where I put my keys. Over *there* is where I put my bag.

While I'm on the topic: Wives, you need to understand that a man has his drop spots, and they are important. I know they might be in the center of the room, but that is planned. That is calculated.

I go to the same spot every time I'm looking for my orange bag. Sure, that spot is essentially in the middle of the kitchen, but that's where I put my bag. And if it's not there, I'll yell forlornly, "Where is my orange bag? Why is my orange bag not here? I left it here. It should still be here."

And the voice of reason and order who shares my home with me will say, "It's in the closet where it belongs."

"But . . . no . . . that's not where it belongs. That's not the drop spot."

Story of my life.

Anyway, home is where you have drop spots. Home is where you smile at the toilet. Home is where you are greeted by nostalgic smells. Home is where you belong, where you let down, where you finally take off the Spanx.

For the record, I haven't worn Spanx in a long time. To God be the glory.

It is amazing how necessary home is. You can travel the world, but you can only be gone so long before you crave home, before you genuinely need to come home. Emotionally and psychologically, I think we all need an identified space, a literal place that we call home, in order to stay sane and healthy and balanced.

We all need to come home. And that leads me to the point of this entire book.

IS IT WELL WITH YOUR SOUL?

A while back I was thinking about this concept of home. I started wondering, *If my physical body needs to regularly go home in order to be healthy, what about my soul? Does my soul have a home? If this tangible, three-dimensional, external body needs a space to simply let down and be itself, what about the inside me?*

Then I asked myself one last question: *When was the last time my soul was at home?*

They were odd questions. Random musings in a moment of melancholy. But they ended up taking me on a journey that changed my approach to God and life. It became an exploration and discovery of how to live the healthy, fulfilled life that I believe God wants us to have.

The more I studied the ramifications and implications of the soul in Scripture, the more I realized our souls are central to our existence, and a healthy soul is paramount to a healthy life.

You can have millions in the bank, a Maserati in the driveway, and more Instagram followers than the pope, but unless your soul is healthy, you won't be happy. The pope actually is on Instagram, in case you were wondering. But I don't think he's on Snapchat. Too bad. I would add him if he had an account—that would be amazing.

But you get the point.

Conversely, you might be struggling through the most painful, confusing circumstances of your life, but if your soul is in a healthy place, you will be okay. You will find the strength and hope you need to weather the storms.

There is a letter in the New Testament known to us as 3 John that references the health of our souls. It was written, not surprisingly, by the apostle John. This was the John who labeled himself "the disciple that Jesus loved" in the gospel of John. I wrote about him and his nickname in my book *Life Is _____*. He had no problem believing that he was special, that he was loved and accepted, that he was God's favorite. He defined himself by how much God loved him. I think if every one of us adopted that attitude, it would solve a lot of the internal turmoil we face.

On a side note, I think I'm going to adapt and adopt his nickname for the Seattle Seahawks. "The team that Jesus loves." Has a nice ring to it.

John wrote 3 John to a man named Gaius, who was a Christian, a friend, and possibly a church leader. John wrote, "Beloved, I pray that all may go well with you and that you may be in good health, as it goes well with your soul" (verse 2).

The Message Bible paraphrases the verse like this: "We're the best of friends, and I pray for good fortune in everything you do, and for your good health—that your everyday affairs prosper, as well as your soul!"

It's a tiny verse in a tiny epistle, tucked away at the tail end of the New Testament—but don't let that fool you. Embedded in this verse is a truth that we will spend the rest of our lives understanding and applying: Each of us has a *soul*. And that soul should be *healthy*.

I've read this verse quite a few times in my life, and I've heard it preached about more than once. If you are a Jesus follower and have been around church awhile, you probably have too.

Usually the application is this: God wants to bless you. God wants to give you health. God wants to give you enough money for your needs, plus some extra to share with others. God wants to prosper you externally just like he's prospered you internally.

Those applications are good and true. I agree with all those things. But in this application, we often take for granted that our souls are healthy. That's a given. We assume that once we are saved, forgiven, and accepted by God, the "inside us" is taken care of. We have peace with God, so we must have peace with ourselves. We are right before God, so we must be right inside ourselves . . . right? And we move on to the rest of the verse.

But is it well with our souls? Is the inside us really steady and stable and secure? Do we ever stop to think about that?

I believe with all my heart that God desires that we have happy, awesome, successful lives. But I am a bit concerned that in our excitement about prospering in our "everyday affairs," as *The Message* puts it, we can end up glossing over the part about the health of our souls.

And that is a problem.

First and foremost, God wants our *souls* to be well. That's why John prays that it would go well with our physical, external selves just as it goes well with our souls.

Actually, this verse seems to imply that until our souls are healthy and prospering, nothing else can prosper. In other words, our health and wellness don't move from the outside in, but from the inside out.

We can be the most popular, prosperous, pretty people around, but inside we can still be empty. Until our souls are at peace, until our souls are stable, until our souls are healthy, those external things won't bring us the satisfaction we long for.

Are our souls healthy? That is the question we should be asking.

Our physical bodies get a lot of attention, of course. We get annual checkups. We go to the dentist. We sign up for hot yoga and CrossFit and Pilates and pretend we like them. Similarly, our bank accounts and vehicles and children and lawns get regular attention. We invest in healthy finances, healthy families, healthy education, and healthy bodies.

But we rarely, if ever, focus on our souls. We don't have routine soul checkups. We don't go around asking each other, "So, how's your soul?" But maybe we should.

I love the idea that things can go well with our souls—that our souls should prosper. Deep inside, isn't that what we are all looking for? We have an innate, intuitive sense that we were designed to be at peace both inside and out. Somehow we sense that happiness, fulfillment, satisfaction, joy, rest, and love are supposed to be the natural state of the human race.

But often our reality lags far behind that ideal. There is pain around us and chaos within us. We struggle to stay at peace. We fight to find happiness. We long for inner rest. We feel out of alignment on the inside, and we aren't quite sure how to set ourselves straight.

Our typical fix when we find problems on the inside is redoubling our efforts on the outside. Maybe you've tried this.

It's far too easy to make life all about the outside me, the external me, the physical me. We fall into the trap that if we can be healthy, wealthy, popular, productive, and influential, then life will be good. So we throw ourselves into the chase, thinking that internal happiness will come from external success. If we just try hard enough, if we just wait long enough, if we just reach the next level, we will feel at peace.

There are two common outcomes to this approach, and both are rather depressing. Excuse my pessimism while I make a point—I promise things will get more cheerful in a moment.

In the first outcome, you try as hard as you can to fix whatever circumstances are messing with your happiness, only to discover eventually that you can't. You can't overcome the leukemia. You can't change your cheating spouse. You can't bring back the loved one you lost. You can't get the job you've built your future around.

So you give up. You resign yourself to a reality that you'd rather avoid. You start living for the weekend. You take up a hobby or maybe an addiction. You figure out ways to escape. You live for moments of happiness that punctuate an otherwise frustrating existence.

The second outcome might even be worse. In this scenario, you actually achieve your goals.

How can that be worse? you might ask.

Because you get what you always wanted, only to discover that it doesn't make you feel any better. Your bank account is full, but you are still empty. And not only that, now the only hope that you could achieve satisfaction is gone, because if anyone on earth should be happy, it's you—and you're not. So what reason is there to go on living?

As I said, I'm making a point here. I don't mean to imply that all humanity is lost, hopeless, and suicidal. But as I've pastored people over the years, I've seen these two scenarios play out more times than I can count.

But it doesn't have to be that way.

When God designed life, he had far more in mind for us than simply surviving. Our existence isn't meant to revolve around escaping reality. We shouldn't live for the weekend, for retirement, or even for heaven.

Those things are great, of course. And living with the end in mind—especially heaven—will help us shape our present. I'm actually going to talk about that later in this book.

But the more I read the Bible and the more I get to know Jesus, the more I realize that this life—even with all its quirks and turns and tragedies—is meant to be amazing. Not because circumstances are always perfect, but because our souls have found their homes in God. Fulfillment comes from having a healthy soul, and as we'll see in a moment, our souls stay healthy when they regularly return home.

THE INSIDE YOU

Before we continue, let's return to the foundational question of what exactly we mean when we refer to "the soul." We've already said that it basically is who we are on the inside, but I want to dig a little deeper. The term *soul* is notoriously hard to define. How can we quantify and categorize something that is invisible, subjective, and untestable? We can't see our souls, so we tend to have trouble even describing them, much less actively caring for them.

And yet, on some level, we are always aware of our souls. We continually monitor whether we are experiencing peace or anxiety, joy or desperation, fulfillment or emptiness.

We say things like, "I really need a vacation" or "This job is sucking the life out of me" or "When I go hiking, I feel alive. I feel renewed." (I would never in a million years say that last one, just for the record. I don't do well with dirt or sweat or the great outdoors in general. I'm more of a mall guy. I buy hiking boots because they look amazing, not because I intend to actually hike in them. But I'm trying to relate to a broader audience, so I threw it in there. You're welcome.)

Anyway, statements like these reflect our souls. They are expressions not just of external, physical conditions but of internal realities. We know that deep inside of us, there is an inner us. We each have an invisible personality and being that is actually more real than our visible, tangible bodies. Even if we can't define it, we know there is something on the inside. We are more than simply the sum of our body parts and brain synapses.

Psychology attempts to define and deal with the inside us,

and considering the complexity of the task, I think it does a great job. I have no problem with psychologists, psychiatrists, philosophers, counselors, mentors, or coaches. I've been to professional counseling on more than one occasion, and I'm sure I could use a few more visits. My wife, Chelsea, would agree.

But for those of us who are Jesus followers, we are especially interested in what the Bible has to say about our souls. We want to learn how to have healthy souls all the time. We want to know how to respond to the ups and downs of life. We want to figure out how to process the fact that our football team lost the Super Bowl by throwing an interception on the 1-yard line and now we can't seem to get out of bed or really even find a reason to live at all. Hypothetically speaking, of course.

The Bible mentions the word *soul* hundreds of times, which is an indicator of how important the subject is to God. The Old Testament often uses the word *heart* to express a similar concept. We are not given one specific definition, however, that fits every scenario.

Commentators who are blessed with far more brain cells than I was given have attempted to quantify and define the soul in exhaustive detail. I'm not going to try to repeat what they say here. Nor am I going to split theological hairs about the difference between the terms *soul* and *spirit*. Sometimes the two seem to be differentiated in Scripture, and sometimes they seem to be synonymous. I'm pretty sure God has it figured out, so I'm not going to lose sleep over it.

I think the phrase "the inside you" does a good job communicating the biblical meaning of the soul. King David wrote,

"Bless the LORD, O my soul, and all that is within me, bless his holy name!" (Psalm 103:1). Note the little phrase "all that is within me." My soul is the center of who I am. It is the inner me, the real me, the invisible me that transcends the physical me, the part of me that in some sense will live eternally in heaven.

BORROWED BREATH

So if our souls are the "inside us," what are we supposed to do about our souls? How do they work? What do they need? How do we know if they are functioning properly? And if they aren't, what can we do about it? Those are a few of the questions we are going to explore throughout this book.

Let's start, appropriately enough, with the beginning of the human soul. The origin of our souls says a lot about how our souls were meant to function. Look at Genesis 2:7: "Then the LORD God formed the man of dust from the ground and breathed into his nostrils the breath of life, and the man became a living creature."

Think about that verse for a moment. Adam's body was created first, but it was by definition lifeless. It was a corpse. His system had not been booted up. The lights had not come on yet. He was merely a shell or a form. He was not alive.

When did mankind become alive? When—and only when—God breathed into him. At that moment Adam became a living creature, a living soul.

That is incredibly significant. God's breath is the essential characteristic of the human soul. Anytime we speak of the human soul, we are speaking of God's breath. The two are inextricably connected. There was no human soul until God breathed, so God's breath defines the human soul.

If God's breath created our souls, then we are literally living on borrowed breath. Whenever we breathe, speak, or sing, we do so because God's life has given life to our souls.

This is more than just poetry or metaphor. This is intensely and immediately practical.

Our souls came from, depend on, and long for God. He gave us life, so his presence is essential to our ongoing health. God's breath is the oxygen our souls breathe. Our souls long for God on a fundamental, foundational level because his life-breath created us and sustains us.

I don't know where you are in respect to God. That's a very personal issue, one that is between you and God. Maybe you don't know much about God. You might doubt if the Bible is really true. You might not be sure what you believe or why you believe it. You might be troubled by all the evil in the world, by the contradictions you perceive in religion, or by the competing philosophies that surround us.

That's okay. I've felt all those things, and I certainly don't have it all figured out. But as I said in the introduction, we are all on a journey in our relationship with God. Luckily we don't have to have it all figured out to start that journey.

But I can say this: when I am honest with myself, I intuitively understand that my inner being is drawn in a strange—but very real—way to a being who is bigger and higher and greater than I am.

My soul wants to come home to God.

If you find in your heart a longing for God, then you are in the right place. You are on the journey, and God will help you find him and find yourself in him. Whether you and I agree on what we think about the Bible and God and sin and heaven is not the issue—the issue is that we are drawing closer to God.

FINDING HOME

A while back I met a friend in Los Angeles who had just recently decided to become a follower of Jesus. He started telling me about his journey.

I asked, "How did you know this was right? How did you make the decision to love Jesus and honor him as God in your life?"

He answered, "The book of John."

That wasn't what I expected. I thought he was going to say he went to church and heard about Jesus, or a friend prayed with him, or something like that. So I said, "Explain."

He told me he had been involved in another religion, but when he read the book of John and read the stories of Jesus, he just knew. This was right. Something inside of him said, *I'm home. This is my home. This is what I was designed for. This is what I've been searching for.*

I've met many people who are emotionally and internally nomadic. They are restless. They have literal, physical homes, but internally they are unsettled. They are always searching for home.

It's an epidemic, if we are really honest. I'm sure we've all felt it. People use phrases like "I'm trying to find myself." They go to extraordinary lengths and spend enormous amounts of money trying to find themselves.

"I don't feel this. I have a job, but this isn't me. I just need to find . . . something. This marriage isn't for me. I'm going to try again. I'm going to change. I'm going to move to a new city. Get a new life. Start over."

There is something inside of you and me that is constantly traveling—here, there, and everywhere—looking for something. That is exactly what was happening in my friend's life until he cracked open the Bible and read the book of John. And then the soul inside of him said, *This is what you have been looking for these thirty years.*

And he came home. Instantly. He didn't change where he was physically, but everything changed internally.

I live in the Pacific Northwest, which happens to be the breeding ground for several species of salmon. If you are in Seattle during July and August, you can visit the Ballard Locks and watch salmon swim up a fish ladder that joins the salt water of the ocean with the freshwater of Lake Washington. Amazingly, these salmon have spent their entire adult lives—usually several years—in the ocean, but they instinctively know how to return to their birthplaces in streams and rivers far up in the mountains. They have a driving passion to return home.

At that point the analogy breaks down, because after the fish return home and spawn, they get eaten by bears and stuff. That's not my point here, so try to erase that mental image.

What I'm saying is that even salmon have a built-in desire

to go back to where they started. They don't stop. They fight any obstacle. They face contrary currents and wild creatures and dams, all in order to return home.

Maybe nature is teaching us something. Maybe the reason we feel restless on the inside is because we haven't been home in a long time. Maybe it's because instinctively, intuitively, and subconsciously we are driven to return to our place of origin: God.

So to repeat my question from the beginning of the chapter, When are our souls home? It's simple.

Our souls are home when they return to God.

That is the purpose, premise, and promise of this book. We were created by God and for God, and we will find ourselves most fully when we find ourselves in him and turn our attention toward him.

Returning to God is the essence of worship. Worship isn't singing or chanting. It isn't rites or rituals or religious traditions. Those things might help us focus on God, but ultimately we must find God himself. Our souls must learn to lean on him and lean into him.

In the next few pages, we will look together at how to have a soul that is healthy and at home. It's a journey that will change your life forever, because as you turn your heart, soul, mind, and emotions toward God, you will find fulfillment on a deeper level—a soul level, a heart level. You will discover the satisfaction and stability that comes from finding your way home.

Your soul is healthiest when it comes back frequently and wholeheartedly to God. That is when you are most alive. That is when you are most human.

That is when you are home.

two

ORIGINAL HOME

I am a healthy eater, or at least I like to think I am. Now that I've hit my midthirties and am heading irreversibly toward my forties, I can't get away with all the carbs and refined sugars I used to eat. I want to be healthy, and I want my wife to think I'm sexy. Those are my main motivations for nutritional eating.

But that's not easy—and probably not for the reasons you would think. You might expect me to say that I love donuts or burgers or milkshakes. That I find creative ways to justify not exercising. That I like to sleep in and skip breakfast. That I tend to eat too late at night. That I drink too many of my calories.

And . . . you might be right on a few of those. But they aren't the real reason it's hard to eat healthy.

The real reason is that I don't *know* what's healthy. I am so confused and lost about what is good for me. I am overwhelmed by the minutia and the blogs and the books and the opinions. Even my nearest and dearest friends can't agree.

For instance, I am a child of the eighties, so a nutritional breakfast growing up included things like Kellogg's Frosted Mini-Wheats. This particular cereal had *wheat* in the name, so it had to be healthy. That was the reasoning.

If it wasn't Mini-Wheats, it was Raisin Bran. Again, the term *bran* automatically gave my mom the assurance she needed that we were eating healthy. Plus it contained raisins, which were descendants of actual fruit, so we knew our breakfast was nutritious.

If it had wheat or bran in the name, we sliced bananas on it and ate it. That was the breakfast philosophy of 1988. We thought it was healthy, so we were happy.

Imagine my shock when, years later, I was informed that Raisin Bran actually has far more sugar in it than those "unhealthy" cereals that we demonize, like Fruit Loops or Frosted Flakes. Turns out those two scoops of former fruit are absolutely caked in refined sugar. Like eighteen grams of it. So now I won't touch the stuff. And I would rather eat the cardboard box of Frosted Mini-Wheats than the cereal inside.

Back in the eighties we avoided butter and bacon because they were fattening. But times have changed. Now I put butter in my coffee and I crush bacon for every meal, because I am bulletproof. That is the newest diet craze. Ironically I used to warn people about bacon. Why? Because pigs don't sweat. Let that sink in for a second. We are eating all their toxins. But now suddenly it's good fat, so we are all about avocados and bacon and butter, and we feel so good about ourselves.

But of course, the World Health Organization recently released a study that appeared to link bacon to an increased risk of certain cancers.[1] That sparked an entire controversy about the nature and level of risk, and people started hashtagging their breakfast photos #bacongate and #freebacon because anyone with taste buds prefers the version of reality that says bacon is healthy.

I am officially 100 percent confused.

Do you remember in the eighties how a candy bar and a milkshake were treats you only got on Saturdays? Now they are meal replacements. They are packed with the perfect proportion of minerals and nutrients and vitamins and calories and good fats and everything else we are supposed to need. So we are all living on shakes and bars because we are high-powered healthy professionals who don't have time for a meal.

Let's be honest: If we are replacing meals, we are leaving out a lot more than food. Many of the best moments of life revolve around friends and food. On what planet is meal replacement a healthier way to live?

I could go on. How about bananas? The other day I was eating a banana, and one of my friends said, "Wow, are you actually eating a banana?" His tone was a mixture of disdain and concern, which confused me.

"Well, yes. I was hungry, and bananas are healthy."

"You might as well have a can of soda."

I was like, "Excuse me? I didn't know bananas were carbonated and filled with corn syrup."

He said, "Your body processes a banana the same way as a can of Coke. You're killing yourself, buddy."

Or what about kale? Kale didn't even exist in 1988. Someone made it up, and that person has made a lot of money on it too.

If we are confused about what is healthy for our bodies, how much more confused are we about what is healthy for our souls? It's relatively easy to measure and analyze the outside us. But what about the inside us? How do we know if we are healthy? How do we become healthy? How do we stay healthy?

In the previous chapter, we looked at God's original design for our souls and concluded that our souls can be healthy only when they are at home in God; that is, when they return to God, when they find their purpose in God, and when they return to relationship with God. We used the word *worship* to refer to that place of intimacy and closeness to our Creator.

In the next few chapters, I want to dive a little deeper into how we can be healthy on the inside. We will be looking at a number of needs and facets of the human soul.

The good news is that this is actually *less* confusing and subjective than all the banana, bacon, and breakfast cereal debates, because we aren't on our own in this process. We don't have to sort through books and blogs and opinions. The Creator himself has given us a handbook for a healthy soul: the Bible.

As we get started, I want to take a look at the original environment of the human soul. In other words, what is the atmosphere that is most helpful for the human soul? What was the setting and context that God originally designed for us?

We are creatures of our environment, after all. Whether we are working, relaxing, or romancing, environment matters. Setting and ambience and mood lighting and the proper sound track make all the difference.

In the beginning, God set humanity in an environment

conducive to internal success. When we look at what the Bible says about the conditions God originally created for the human soul, we discover a blueprint and a plan to achieve soul health. I want to look at what I think are the four essential elements of that environment. You can still exist without them, of course—many people do—but they are essential if we are going to get the most out of life.

Remember, God is the designer, the architect, and the originator of this complicated entity called the human soul. When he created the soul, he placed it in an optimal environment, in a place where it could thrive. Why? Because God wants us to thrive in life. He didn't create us to barely make it or merely survive. He wants to help us have healthy souls and full lives. If we can implement these elements in our everyday lives, I believe we will be healthy to our cores. Even when our *outside* environments aren't particularly healthy or stable, if we are healthy on the *inside*, we will conquer adversity.

NO, MINE, GIMME, NOW

Before we look at the four elements of a healthy soul environment, I should mention that these things were part of God's *original* creation for humankind, and this creation did not include the presence of evil. When God designed the soul, evil did not exist; death did not exist; selfishness did not exist. Humanity enjoyed a sinless, flawless environment.

That is not true anymore, in case you haven't noticed. Babies do not spring from the womb thinking, *I want to love and share and give.* Quite the opposite. If you have kids and they are anything like mine, their first few words included terms like *no, mine, gimme,* and *now.* Often in that order and at a deafening decibel level to boot.

Everywhere we look we see the effects of evil. Wars, genocide, racism, terrorism, greed, destruction—while governments and military forces in every nation try to limit evil, they can't eradicate it, because it springs from within us.

Sorry to sound so negative. But it's essential that we understand that sin was not part of God's creation. Why? Because if we try to apply these four elements to our souls without dealing with the sin issue, it won't work. They will be lifeless and empty because, as we saw before, the most important thing we can do for a healthy soul is to come into a relationship with God.

How is that possible? How can we who were born on a hurting planet, a planet suffering under the influence and pull of evil, be restored to the purity that God originally created?

It is clear throughout human history that we cannot solve the sin problem on our own. We cannot become good again through self-effort; we cannot achieve right standing with God based on our performance.

That is why God sent his Son, Jesus. The Bible says that "God put the wrong on him who never did anything wrong, so we could be put right with God" (2 Corinthians 5:21 THE MESSAGE).

As we relate to God from a place of forgiveness and acceptance through Jesus, we can apply these four elements to our lives. We can surround ourselves with this kind of environment, and we will experience the health and happiness that God gives our souls.

ENJOY THE TREES

We see the first element of a healthy soul environment in Genesis 2:7–9.

Verse 7 describes the creation of humanity this way: "Then the LORD God formed the man of dust from the ground and breathed into his nostrils the breath of life, and the man became a living creature." We looked at this verse in the previous chapter, and we saw that when God breathed his soul-breath into Adam's lifeless body, Adam became a living soul.

Then, starting with verse 8, there is a description of the optimum, soul-nurturing environment that God created for mankind. It just might surprise you.

> And the LORD God planted a garden in Eden, in the east, and there he put the man whom he had formed. And out of the ground the LORD God made to spring up every tree that is pleasant to the sight and good for food. (verses 8–9)

Remember, this is the most ideal environment God could have designed. It was the original home for the human soul, a place where our souls, spirits, and hearts would thrive.

It's not nearly as spiritual as you might think. I would have expected angels singing softly in the treetops, or worship music playing in the background, or engravings of Bible verses posted on trees, or at least a statue of God somewhere.

But the first thing God wants us to know about the original environment is that the trees were beautiful and they had delicious fruit.

Excuse me, God?

Consider what God is saying here. It seems so arbitrary—but it's not. He's sending us a message about what our souls need.

Our souls need *rest*. They need relaxation, enjoyment, peace, and pleasure.

If we polled people and asked them what they thought religion and a relationship with God was all about, what do you think they would say? I think many would answer, "It's about rules. About morals. About keeping the Ten Commandments. About behaving and being good." And if they were honest, I think many would continue, "Actually, I should probably go back to church. I feel bad. I feel guilty. My life's not right. I think God is mad at me."

Here's what I *don't* think a lot of people would say: "Relationship with God? It's about enjoying God. It's about enjoying life, nature, good food, and friends. It's about rest. Rest is what God wants for my life."

Yet God gives us a picture of rest by saying, "Enjoy the sights and the tastes. I want you to love it. It's free. It's for you. I designed life to be enjoyable."

In our fixation with keeping rules and appeasing a God we secretly suspect might be angry or disappointed, we are in danger of losing one of the fundamental keys to a healthy soul: that of rest, of enjoying who God is and what he has created for us. God wants to remind us how imperative rest and enjoyment are for our souls, so the first description we get of the garden is that the foliage is fun to look at and the food tastes amazing.

Why is rest first? Rest is first because God is first. A restless soul is a soul that thinks it is in control and needs to take care of everything. If we do not rest, we are trying to be our own God. We have to remember that even when we rest, God does not. When we sleep, God does not. And when we cease working, God does not.

I think God was communicating to Adam, "You know that none of this was because of you, right? I created all of this on my own and I gave it to you, so don't take yourself too seriously there, slugger. Okay? This is something I did. I made you too. So you are not God. It's not all on you. I love you, and I made you just for me. So how about you enjoy the trees, eat some fruit, and relax a little bit. You're not that big of a deal, just FYI."

It's amazing how big of a deal we become in our own minds sometimes. It leads to so much anxiety and fear.

Do you know where worry comes from? From thinking we are in control. True rest is unattainable for people who are obsessed with leading their own lives. But rest is one of the primary postures of those who know Jesus, because we have a God who is in control and who is taking care of us.

Psalm 127:1–2 describes how useless it is to overburden ourselves with the cares and concerns of life:

> Unless the LORD builds the house,
> those who build it labor in vain.

*Unless the L*ORD *watches over the city,*
  the watchman stays awake in vain.
It is in vain that you rise up early
  and go late to rest,
eating the bread of anxious toil;
  for he gives to his beloved sleep.

This is so applicable to modern culture. He is saying, "It's pointless for you to work late into the night. To skip sleep, to wake up early in the morning and start working again, as if you were in control and you were the only provider and protector for your life."

Where is the margin in that? Where is the rest? Where are the awareness and acknowledgment of your Creator and your Designer who is sovereign over life's unpredictability?

The songwriter says, "You can't even enjoy the bread in your mouth because you are so worried you won't have enough money to buy another loaf tomorrow." He might as well be talking about those meal replacement bars. Some people can never enjoy a good meal with good friends because they are so important and so busy.

Somehow I don't think that's what God had in mind for the human soul when he created the garden of Eden. The original home of the soul had great-looking trees and awesome food—that gives us a little bit of perspective, doesn't it? Maybe what we are here for is not to be so important, successful, awesome, and busy that we don't even have time to eat. Let's enjoy God and enjoy his creation.

One of the most spiritual things you can do today might be to cancel your fast-paced, anxious preparation for your big meeting tomorrow. Make a new friend or look up some old friends and go get some good food. Take time to laugh about life and consider the goodness of God.

Maybe you are worried or fearful about something, and you think, *I need to fast and pray.* That might be a great thing to do. There is a time and place for that. But sometimes even spiritual activity can be a subconscious attempt to make things happen. Sometimes the best option is to share a meal with a friend who's gone through something similar. Let him or her process with you, cry with you, and laugh with you. Don't get too overwhelmed. Lean into God and trust that he really is looking out for you.

Jesus said, "Come to me, all who labor and are heavy laden, and I will give you rest. Take my yoke upon you, and learn from me, for I am gentle and lowly in heart, and you will find rest for your souls" (Matthew 11:28–29). He couldn't have been any clearer. Our souls need rest, and he is our ultimate source of rest.

"He gives to his beloved sleep," Psalm 127:2 says. I have to be honest: that is one of my favorite verses in the Bible.

Sometimes God just wants you to go to bed. When is the last time you heard a preacher say that? Sometimes the most spiritual, godly, and God-aware thing you can do is take a nap. Realize you probably won't figure it all out or get it all done, but God is with you and God is for you.

WORK IT

The second element of a healthy soul environment is found in Genesis 2:15. "The LORD God took the man and put him in the garden of Eden to work it and keep it." In other words, God gave the human soul *responsibility*.

This could be shocking to some people, because they assume that work was the result of sin. They think that God gave Adam a job as punishment because he messed up. "Adam, clearly you have too much time on your hands, and that's why you are running around getting into trouble. So guess what. I just invented something called *work*. You'll hate it, you'll resent it, but you're stuck with it."

That's the attitude the American culture often seems to take. Some of us think, *I will get a job because I need to have a job, but I'm going to work the job as hard as I can so that someday I can quit that job.*

Why? Because we think a responsibility-free environment will make us happier. We assume that since work is hard but vacation is fun, work itself is the problem. Responsibility is an intruder. Jobs are the enemy. We work hard so that someday we can retire and start to do what we actually enjoy.

Yet the second element in the Bible's description of this original, sin-free environment is that God had an assignment for Adam. He had a job. The difference is that before the intrusion of sin, there was no anxiety, toil, or sweat in that job. But Adam still had something he was required to do. God created humans to bear responsibility.

The Hebrew word translated *work* here can also be rendered *serve*.[2] Often when we think about serving, we think in terms of sacrifice, but serving actually benefits the servant the most. Serving makes your soul feel good. It makes you feel alive on the inside. Your soul finds fulfillment, health, and life when you live beyond yourself.

Responsibility is good for the soul. I sound like my dad right now, but it's true. Sometimes we equate a lack of responsibility with living free, but that's not freedom. That's not how our souls operate. We need assignments, we need work, and we need activity.

Some people want responsibility, but they only want the task they want. And if they don't get the job or role or assignment they want, then they don't take it to heart. They think, *When I get that dream job, I will care enough to really give myself to it; but right now, I don't really care. I hate my job, so I'll do the least possible amount of work to get my paycheck.*

The Bible says, "Whatever your hand finds to do, do it with all your might" (Ecclesiastes 9:10 NIV). Have you ever stopped to think that maybe responsibility is a key to fulfillment and joy on the inside? Maybe soul satisfaction is tied more to responsibility itself than to a particular role or a dream job.

I started working at the City Church as a custodian. It wasn't my preference, but I wanted to work at the church, and one day a custodial position opened up. So I took it.

I'm sure I was not the best custodian. I definitely missed some stuff. And I will never clean another women's bathroom, because I'm scarred for life. But that's beside the point. I will say, though, that I think I had the most fun of any custodian ever in my church. No matter who was working with me, we always had a blast. We laughed the whole time. And it sounds crazy, but I found so much fulfillment in that job.

What's even crazier is this: now I'm in charge of the whole

church, but it hasn't made me any happier. Being the lead pastor as opposed to a custodian has not increased my joy level one bit. I was happy before and I'm happy now. I was tempted to be worried and fearful and insecure before, and I face the same temptations now. The things that people would call success have not given me more joy, peace, or security on the inside.

What has given me joy, whether I'm the custodian or the lead pastor, is that I do it with all my heart. The joy is not in the role. The joy is in the responsibility.

I am responsible for this job, I decided. *This is my world. These are my bathrooms to clean. This is my lobby to vacuum. I'm going to do this, and I'm going to sing and rap the whole time, and I'm going to write sermons in my head, and I'm going to have an awesome time.*

Don't wait for a certain role to come along. Your soul's happiness and health are not dependent upon a role. Your soul was designed to do whatever you do with everything within it. It needs responsibility to be healthy, and there is a good chance that responsibility is right in front of you.

A NECESSARY NO

The next element of an environment that helps our souls to thrive appears in Genesis 2:16–17 (NIV).

> And the LORD God commanded the man, "You are free to eat from any tree in the garden; but you must not eat from the

tree of the knowledge of good and evil, for when you eat from
it you will certainly die."

It's indicative of God's grace that he gave permission before
restriction. He said, "You can eat from every tree except one."
How many trees were there? Hundreds? Thousands? Adam and
Eve could eat from all of them except one: the tree of the knowledge of good and evil.

Think about that. The odds were stacked in their favor. God
wasn't trying to trap them. He didn't give them impossible com-
mands and then laugh when they failed. He made it as simple
and straightforward as possible. He set them up for success.

He gave them the world, but he gave them limits too.

At this point, a lot of people say, "It's God's fault. If God would
not have put that one little bad tree in the garden, we wouldn't be
in this predicament today. Why didn't he leave that tree out?"

First, without that tree, we lose our definition of love. Love
requires free will. If there is no choice in love, then it isn't love.
Forced love is how you end up in jail. God is love, and he created us to be loved and to love. But we had to have the power of
choice to respond to him. There had to be real options, a real
opportunity to choose or reject God, or it wouldn't be love and it
wouldn't be free will.

I want to focus, however, on another reason I believe this
tree was placed in the garden. It is the third element of a healthy
environment: *restraint*. Restriction and restraint are necessary
for a healthy soul.

I really sound like my parents now. Maybe that's because

I've been a parent for twelve years and counting. Often I find myself saying no to my kids simply because no is what is needed. I might have the means to meet their request. I might even have the desire to meet it. But I say no because that is what my son or daughter needs in the moment.

Sometimes there is a clear reason why I have to say no. Other times there isn't, but somehow I still know the answer needs to be no. They need the limits; they need the restraints and constraints.

A child who never hears no becomes "that kid." We all know "that kid." Likewise, if we don't have limits we can become "that man" or "that woman." A soul without restraints is an unhealthy soul, and the results are obvious to those around us.

I believe God put the tree of the knowledge of good and evil there because when Adam and Eve walked by, the limitation was good for their souls. Their souls felt protected and secure. Their souls felt directed and guarded because they had the ability to say, "I can, but I won't; and that's good for me."

Growing up, my parents held the "*no* card" for my sister and me. Now I hold it for my kids. Guess what maturity is all about? Guess what parenting is all about? Leading our kids to a place where they can say no for themselves, even when they want to say yes.

That's the challenge: self-imposed restraint. That is maturity in a nutshell. It's when you have the money, you have the desire, you have the opportunity, and yet you still say, "Nope."

Why? Because sometimes you need to hear yourself tell yourself no. *That was good for me*, your soul will say. Don't underestimate how significant a no is for the health of your soul.

Maria Montessori was an Italian educator whose educational system and philosophy greatly affected US education. Her educational process was predicated upon the belief that children were in their optimal educational environment when they had freedom within limits.[3]

Freedom within limits. That would be the garden of Eden. That is where the soul is at its best.

God designed restrictions and limitations as a blessing for your soul. You and I are not God. We need constraints and restraints. We need checks and balances.

God knows that, of course, and he built restraints into the form and function of every facet of life. Contrary to popular belief, not all rules are made to be broken and not all limits are meant to be tested. We need to grow in maturity until we can distinguish what restraints are healthy and submit ourselves to those restraints.

HELPERS WHO FIT

These first three elements—rest, responsibility, and restraint— fall flat if we miss the last element: *relationship.*

Genesis 1, the first chapter of the Bible, recounts the six days of creation. Sun, moon, stars, earth, plants, animals, man— everything was incredible. God looked at his work after each stage of creation, and he saw that it was good (verses 10, 12, 18, 21, 25). When he finished, the Bible says he looked over all creation and "it was very good" (verse 31). In fact, it was so good that

God decided to take the seventh day off. Not because he was tired, but because he was finished.

But there was one thing in that perfect, sinless, universe that was *not* good. "The LORD God said, 'It is not good for the man to be alone. I will make a helper suitable for him'" (Genesis 2:18 NIV).

In other words, even though Adam's soul was perfect, it was not healthy for it to be alone. Not only that, but God personally was going to provide companionship and relationship.

We are, by nature, relational beings. We were meant for community. Even the most introverted, solitary personality types need at least some level of human interaction in order to maintain healthy, thriving, vibrant souls. It is unhealthy for our souls to be isolated or without relationship.

This is imperative. Yes, we need rest, we need responsibility, and we need restraint. But more than anything, we need relationship. That's why God himself called an intervention.

God proceeded to create woman, and Adam and Eve became the first married couple and ultimately the parents and progenitors of the entire human race.

Marriage continues to be the single most important human relationship, but I think this passage speaks of more than just marriage. Marriage, in essence, is friendship. Without friendship it is next to impossible to make marriage work.

Let's consider Genesis 2:18 in friendship terms. Look at how involved God is in making a friend for Adam. *Does God care about my friends?* you might wonder. He most definitely does. Just look at this story.

God says, "I will make a helper suitable for him." A healthy friend could be defined as "a helper who fits."

So here are my questions and my appeal to you as we talk about a healthy soul.

Are you intentional about your friends?

Are they helping you?

Do you fit together?

Yes, I think we should live big. We should draw big circles, be inclusive, be forgiving, and be kind—but we can't be intimate friends with all seven billion people on this planet. We can't be close friends with a few thousand people. Probably not even a few hundred people.

Realistically, we might be close, intimate friends with only a dozen people. Maybe a few more or a few less, depending on our individual capacities and personalities. So we had better choose those people intentionally, carefully, and prayerfully.

Someone once said, "Show me your friends, and I'll show you your future." But we could go even further. "Show me your friends, and I will show you the state of your soul." These are the people who are feeding you on the inside.

Are they giving you life?

Are they serving or only taking?

Are they building you up or tearing you down?

Are they healing your soul or hurting your soul?

By the same token, are you providing for the needs of their souls? A healthy friendship is a two-way street.

Consider carefully the relationships in your life. A lot of people take relationships as they come, with little analysis or long-term thought. "You want to hang out every night? Sure! You want to date me? Sounds good! Sleep together? Hey, why not?"

Friendships and relationships are more important than that. Be careful and be intentional. Let God lead you.

I'm talking about close relationships, of course—the people you are doing life with on a consistent basis. I'm not saying to exclude everyone else, or to never be open to new friends. I'm simply saying that if God went to that kind of effort to provide an appropriate friend and companion for Adam, he will help you too. I believe your relationships can be created, ordained, and put together by the hands of God. Those God-given relationships will create an environment where your soul can thrive.

Maybe as you read this, you are thinking to yourself, *I can tell you right now, my soul is not in a healthy place.* Proverbs 18:14 says: "A healthy spirit conquers adversity, but what can you do when the spirit is crushed?" (THE MESSAGE).

What can you do when your spirit is crushed? What can you do when the inside you is broken and unhealthy?

Go to the originator and designer of your soul. Go to the one who gave you breath to begin with, and say, "Okay, God, I'm starting over. I'm starting fresh. I want to be healthy to my core. I want to focus on my soul and my heart, not just my physical body or external circumstances."

God will help you. He'll give you rest. He'll guide you into appropriate responsibilities. He'll surround you with safe restraints. He'll provide relationships that fit and friends who help you navigate the twists and turns and ups and downs of life.

We might not always know what diet plan to follow for healthy bodies, but we have a guide to healthy souls. And as we intentionally and regularly follow God's plan, our souls will be free to thrive.

three

SURPRISED BY MY SOUL

Your soul finds its home in God. It's a beautiful thought.

At least when things are going well.

Like when you're sitting by a pristine lake at sunset on a summer evening and everything is right in the world. At that point, it's easy to believe that God wants your soul to draw close to him. It feels so natural. So perfect. Anyone can be spiritual by a lake.

But unfortunately, we can't live there. I don't mean by a lake—I mean in a glorious and perpetual state of serenity and tranquility. Our souls go through emotional upheavals more often than we'd like to admit. And it's confusing. Shocking. Disconcerting.

For example, I remember when *The Fresh Prince of Bel-Air* changed the character of Aunt Viv. That show was a staple of my childhood years, but about three years in, for no apparent reason, they changed Aunt Viv. I remember watching the first episode of the new season, and I'm like, *Why is he calling her Aunt Viv? That is not Aunt Viv. Lady, you are an imposter. Where is Aunt*

Viv? The first three years it was the real Aunt Viv, and from then on it was the illegitimate Aunt Viv, the non-real Aunt Viv.

Mentally, of course, I knew what had happened. I recall telling myself, *Judah, my goodness, get ahold of yourself. It's a sitcom. It's a TV show. It's not real.*

But I missed Aunt Viv, and I still miss Aunt Viv on the reruns.

Another surprising moment in my apparently overly dramatic childhood was when *Rocky IV* came out. Remember when Ivan Drago killed Apollo Creed? Of course you do. An entire generation of children was instantly and permanently scarred by that movie.

I absolutely could not understand my emotions watching *Rocky IV.* I cried. I punched the air. I yelled at the screen. "You killed Apollo Creed! Are you kidding me? He was my friend!"

It was a movie. I knew that. But clearly I struggled with some intense emotions—and I still do.

Recently Chelsea and I wanted to watch a movie at home. She said, "You pick one." So I started looking through On Demand, and I chose *The Fault in Our Stars.* Obviously I didn't watch the preview.

By the time I figured out it was a tragedy, it was too late. I was already immersed in the calamity and chaos and pain of humanity.

When the movie ended, I looked over at Chelsea. She had fallen asleep, as if we were watching a comedy or something. Apparently my wife doesn't care about the plight of the world.

But I was devastated. I lay there, tears soaking my pillow, and all I could say—and I said it out loud—was, "Man, this planet sucks!" I was so emotional.

I kept trying to tell myself, *These are actors. When the credits roll and the sound track ends, they are going to go on and live prosperous, healthy lives.* But I couldn't shake myself out of my emotional funk.

I woke up the next morning. It was Tuesday, and I had to lead a staff meeting at the church with about a hundred staff members. But I was still in a dark place. I kept asking people, "Have you seen *The Fault in Our Stars?* We have to do something! Life is so painful." So bizarre—I was rallying people to a completely fictional cause. What is wrong with me?

One last example. A while back I played in a golf tournament at our local golf course. I had high hopes and expectations for my performance because I'm an optimist, and against all odds I always believe there is a pro golfer inside me who will manifest someday.

I had a terrible game, to put it bluntly, and I was hurting inside. I held myself together for all eighteen holes, but only because I was playing with legitimate adults. A couple of them knew I was a pastor, unfortunately. So I was like, "Oh wow, a bogie! No big deal. Who cares? Listen to the birds. Look at the blue sky."

It was totally fake. That's not me at all. Who cares about the birds and the sky? I just bogied for the fourth time, and I wanted to die. Or at least cuss. But I played it off like it was no big deal. "It's golf. It's just a game." Inside I was thinking, *No, it's not just a game! It's the most important thing in the universe right now!* But I didn't say that.

I shot an 88, which is bad for me. I knew that my golfing friends would call me and ask me how I played, and I was embarrassed. But I was still playing it cool.

Until I got to my car.

My whole family—Chelsea and our three kids—was waiting for me inside the vehicle. I got in and shut the door. The first thing my five-year-old said was, "Hey, Dad, how did you do?"

That was when I snapped. I lost it. I started punching the dashboard like a loved one had passed away or something. Then between punches I heard my ever-observant eight-year-old say, "Not so good, I guess."

Five minutes later, of course, I was mortified. Shocked by my reactions. Embarrassed by my behavior. *Really, Judah?* I thought. *There is already a five-year-old in this family, and it's not you. It's a golf game. Get some perspective.*

I apologized to my wife and kids. As far as I know, no one I knew walked by during my meltdown. That would have been awkward.

"Pastor? Is that you?"

"Hey, God bless you! I'm just punching my dashboard here. Randomly. Praise God."

Have you ever been surprised by your soul? Shocked by your feelings? Stunned by your reactions?

Do you know what it's like when your emotions are so raw and so real? You can't help yourself. You are in a horrible space, a really low place, because what you are experiencing is so tangible to you.

But a few minutes later, you say to yourself, *My gosh, I thought I was bigger than that. I thought I was more mature than that. I thought I had journeyed a little bit beyond that. But here I am, acting like a child again.*

You feel surprised by your soul—by how badly you feel and how strongly it affects you and controls you. You can't seem to gain perspective in the moment.

The source of pain can be almost anything, by the way—a word, an event, a loss, a fear. It can be big or small or momentary or ongoing. I'm using lighthearted examples here, but I certainly don't mean to gloss over genuine tragedy. My point here isn't so much what triggered the emotional spiral as what to do about it now.

What do you do when your emotions are so out of alignment that you can't see straight? When your thoughts betray you, accuse you, and confuse you? When the world around you and the world within you are equally devoid of hope and happiness? When you find yourself pounding dashboards or grieving the loss of fictional characters?

What do you do when your soul hurts?

OF ROLLER COASTERS AND SCONES

I'm probably the most sentimental member of my family. I'll admit that. Emotional moments are a regular occurrence for me. I don't know if it's hormones or Seattle weather or the fact that my older sister and my mom raised me to like shopping and fashion, and somehow that translated into extreme emotional sensitivity—who knows? All I know is that the inside me is not always as stable as I'd like.

My second-born child appears to be a lot like me, and I feel for him. If you are a parent, you know what I mean. The quirks in your kids that bother you the most are the ones they inherited from you. You recognize them instantly because you've dealt with them your whole life. You just want to warn them, "A dark road awaits you. Turn back now."

Luckily for our emotional selves, there is an entire book of the Bible dedicated to feelings: Psalms. It's about more than just feelings, of course, but emotions definitely play a role in this book.

I think King David, who wrote many of the psalms, was an emotional kind of guy. He was a warrior, he was a king, he was a fighter—but he was also a lover and a poet. He was complicated, just like us.

Psalms 42 and 43 are examples of the kind of soul turmoil that people everywhere experience nearly every day. Most scholars believe these were originally one song rather than two. I'm not going to quote them in their entirety, but they are worth reading if for no other reason than to marvel at the emotional carnage as the psalmist repeatedly climbs out of the depths of despondency only to lose his footing and fall back in. Here are the first six verses:

> As a deer pants for flowing streams,
>   so pants my soul for you, O God.
> My soul thirsts for God,
>   for the living God.
> When shall I come and appear before God?
> My tears have been my food
>   day and night,

while they say to me all the day long,
  "Where is your God?"
These things I remember,
  as I pour out my soul:
how I would go with the throng
  and lead them in procession to the house of God
with glad shouts and songs of praise,
  a multitude keeping festival.

Why are you cast down, O my soul,
  and why are you in turmoil within me?
Hope in God; for I shall again praise him,
  my salvation and my God.

My soul is cast down within me;
  therefore I remember you
from the land of Jordan and of Hermon,
  from Mount Mizar.

The first couple of lines are great. The songwriter sounds spiritual and stable. He's in touch with nature. He's even talking about deer and stuff.

Then suddenly, out of nowhere, he starts screaming. *"When shall I come and appear before God?"* (verse 2). Okay, I added the emphasis. But I'm sure he was yelling at this point.

After a few lines of emotional chaos, he tries to pull himself together. Grabs some Kleenex. Looks around for his man card. Asks himself in verse 5, "Why are you cast down, O my soul?"

He actually repeats this phrase three times in these two psalms (42:5, 11; 43:5). In other words, *Self, what is wrong with you? Soul, why are you so down in the dumps?* He's talking to himself, and we get to listen in.

I think the poet who wrote this song was surprised by his soul. He seems confused by the depth and the violence of his emotions. I love the fact that this is in the Bible, by the way. It validates our own emotional wonderings and wanderings, and I think that's the point.

This is reality. This is human nature. If you have never been surprised by your soul, you are obviously an android, and you are not real. You are a clone. But we humans have those days where we are like, "Wow, I just lost it. I went to Starbucks, and they were out of orange scones, and I went off on the barista. What is wrong with me?"

That didn't happen, but it could. I'm keeping this at scone levels so no one feels picked on.

Another thing to notice here is how many questions the songwriter asks. I count nearly a dozen questions in only sixteen verses. Things like, "When is God going to pay attention to me?" (42:2). "Where is God?" (42:3). "Why has God forgotten me?" (42:9). "Why are my enemies winning?" (42:9).

This is real. This is relatable, because when we are discouraged, we tend to ask a lot of questions. Especially the unanswerable kind—the ones that start with *when* and *why*. Just like the songwriter, we tend to ponder the huge, galactic questions about the existence of God and pain when we are at our lowest points.

That is the worst time to try to answer those questions, by the way. You can ask them, but don't attempt to answer them.

Don't make massive conclusions about the reality or goodness or presence of God in the middle of an emotional meltdown. For that matter, don't take out a loan, get divorced, get married, or do anything else overly life-altering just because your emotions are crying out for escape. In the journey of life, emotions make great companions but terrible leaders.

But anyway, back to our passage. I'm amazed—even comforted, I'll admit—by how many changes of emotional direction there are in these few verses. I counted those as well, and there are at least nine. Nine different times the psalm alternates between positive and negative, between hopeful and depressing, between the heights of happiness and the depths of despair.

When I first noticed the emotional up-and-down nature of this passage, I wondered, *If I could put a sound track to this emotional trajectory, what would it sound like?* Bear with me—this is just how my brain works when I read the Bible. It's chaos.

I concluded that it would probably sound like a roller coaster. So when the psalmist is going up emotionally, when he is relatively controlled and hopeful, that would be represented by the *click-click-click-click* of a roller coaster climbing.

If you've been on any roller coasters, that isn't necessarily the most comforting sound, because we have all heard that what goes up must come down. But at least you aren't *currently* going down. You are going up, thank God, and you can breathe the fresh air and see the countryside or at least the parking lot far below, and no one around you is screaming.

Yet.

Click-click-click.

Then inevitably you reach the top. And you start going down. And everything changes.

The sound track for that portion would be something like this:

Aaaaahhhhhhhh!

Frantic, desperate, panicked screams. Really, the written page doesn't do it justice. I'm looking forward to recording the audiobook for this.

If we replace the text of Psalms 42 and 43 with our sound track, here is what the psalmist's emotional journey would sound like over the course of sixteen verses:

Click, click, click, click,
Aaaaahhhhhhhh!
Click, click, click,
Aaaahhhhh!
Click, click,
Aaaaahhhhhhhh!
Click, click, click,
Aaaaahhhh!
Click, click, click.

He ends on a positive note. Sort of.

Again, this is real life. Some of us, especially those of us who are Jesus followers, want to pretend that life is just *click, click, click* all the time.

"How are you?" someone asks.

"I'm great!" *Click, click, click, click.* "No problems here. No worries or anxiety or depression or confusion of the soul. Why do you ask?" *Click, click, click.*

But the truth is, for normal people, our lives are more like *click, click, aaaahhhhh! click, click, aaaahhhhh! click, click, click, aaaahhhhh!* That's our story all day, every day.

Think about it—when someone asks how your day has been and you reply, "Good," what you are really saying is, "I only went into free fall three or four times today. That's not bad. Bad days are more like ten free falls. So it's been a pretty good day."

I love these two psalms, because this is actually what life on this troubled planet sounds like and feels like. High highs and low lows. You don't even have to be an emotional person. You could be a cerebral person, a math person. Regardless, you are going to feel emotions. We all have them. God gave them to us. And it can be really challenging and alarming when we find ourselves on this pained planet called Earth and we can't seem to find any stability or clarity.

The songwriter's attitude is especially interesting when you realize he was some sort of public figure. Psalm 42, verse 4, says,

> *These things I remember,*
> *as I pour out my soul:*
> *how I would go with the throng*
> *and lead them in procession to the house of God*
> *with glad shouts and songs of praise,*
> *a multitude keeping festival.*

In other words, this is a person with great influence. He says, "I led the people. I led the crowd in praise to the creator God. I had a platform." This would have been in Jerusalem, the capital of Israel. The songwriter was the artist, the public figure, the VIP.

Maybe you aren't a public figure in the Hollywood sense of the word, but you have influence. We all do. So what do we do when we find ourselves leading others externally, but we are unhealthy internally? When we are helping throngs of people, but inside we are weak and unwell?

This songwriter seems to relate to that. Notice what he says in verse 6:

> My soul is cast down within me;
>> therefore I remember you
> from the land of Jordan and of Hermon,
>> from Mount Mizar.

Just listen to his condition and his circumstances. He is saying, "I am nowhere near Jerusalem. That place of success and importance and fame is nothing but a memory. Here I am by this random mountain, wishing I were back there on a platform, leading multitudes of people. Instead, I am far away, and I am not well. I am broken. I am surprised by my own emotions and my own inconsistencies."

This songwriter is facing that dichotomy. He has helped others, but who will help him? He's a leader. He should know better. He should be better. But he's struggling, because he's human too. His popularity and platform only add to the angst, the pain, and the shame.

That sounds a lot like our culture today. It's the paradox of leadership and influence. Just because you lead people and help people doesn't mean you are always going to be healthy on the inside. If anything, the pressure of public influence increases the unhealthy tendencies of our souls. If we aren't careful, it can make us defensive and isolated. Instead of looking for help when we need it, we pretend to have it all together.

HOPE IN GOD

Scriptures like Psalms 42 and 43 remind us that God knows exactly what is going on inside us. God is the master architect of the complicated, confusing, and even contradictory constructs that we call our souls.

Maybe our souls surprise us—but they don't surprise God. He isn't shocked or scandalized by the up-and-down tendencies of our hearts. He isn't embarrassed just because our feelings get out of hand. He sees the craziness and chaos, and it doesn't bother him a bit. He knows us better than anyone, and he loves us more than everyone.

If God designed the human soul, then it's only logical that he would know how to fix it when it is out of alignment. Yet sometimes we are so embarrassed by our emotions and so freaked out by our feelings that we avoid the one who knows our souls the best.

So we try to fix ourselves on our own. But the results are usually underwhelming, because it's surprisingly hard to feel better just because we want to. It's difficult for our souls to pull themselves up by their own bootstraps—whatever bootstraps are—because emotions are so complicated and even subversive.

The problem with discouragement is that discouragement never leads to encouragement. Have you noticed that? Discouragement leads to more discouragement. We are down because we are down. We feel sad about how sad we are. We can't believe that we got so frustrated over a scone or a golf game or Aunt Viv, and the revelation of our immaturity depresses us even more, and the whole thing self-perpetuates.

How do we interrupt the cycle? How do we short-circuit this discouragement that leads to more discouragement until finally we need an intervention just to shake ourselves out of the funk we are in?

This passage shows where the songwriter found his stability and clarity. As we saw earlier, he asks three times, "Why are you cast down, O my soul, and why are you in turmoil within me?"

Each time he asks the question, he comes up with the same answer. It's a definitive, clarifying statement. It's a perspective that pushes away the cloudiness, the murky moments, the confusing feelings.

"Hope in God; for I shall again praise him, my salvation and my God" (42:5, 11; 43:5).

How did he get to that place? We know this: it didn't happen instantaneously. That's obvious just by charting his roller-coaster ride.

Maybe you have been beating yourself up because it has taken you a long time to recover your focus and your faith. You need to stop. I'm pretty sure that's called being human. Don't lose hope just because you've struggled for a while. Notice this: the songwriter is in frantic free fall for four full verses before he comes to himself and says, "Wait a minute—what am I feeling and why am I feeling it?"

Two things stand out in this musician's journey. First, he's willing to question his feelings. *Why am I feeling this way?*

This is incredibly important in today's culture and society. If we want to be healthy on the inside, we have to question our insides. We have to question our souls. We have to question our feelings.

That seems so simple. But we are living in an age where feelings have become the unquestioned, unassailable bastions of individual truth and identity.

Question what I feel? No, that would be disingenuous. Unauthentic. I just need to go with what I feel. Be organic and real and unscripted.

I've been a pastor and speaker for almost two decades now. I can't recall how many times I've sat down with a college dude at a coffeehouse somewhere in Seattle or LA or some other city, and the first thing out of his mouth was, "Well, I just feel . . ."

And I would share a scripture or a thought, and he would respond, "But, Judah, I feel . . ."

Feelings are the language of the day. And telling someone that what they feel might be incorrect is a cardinal sin in our society.

True story: recent research has shown that human beings are irrational.[1] That's not really news to any of us. According to these researchers, we make definitive, moral decisions impulsively and irrationally. And then we spend an inordinate amount of time defending those impulsive, irrational decisions.

We make decisions based on feelings and we call them facts. Why? Because they feel true. *These are really my feelings,* says this logic, *so whatever belief or idea these feelings are attached to must also be true. It feels true to me, so this is my truth, and you had better not tell me it's fiction because that would be to deny the validity and authority of my feelings.*

I'm not being mean to emotional, feelings-oriented people. I am one, remember? I would be totally in favor of this kind of personal, subjective way of living and acting if it *worked*. I would be totally down with this philosophy if it produced lasting joy, fulfillment, and meaning.

But let's look at this logically. What if we all counted to three and then simultaneously did whatever we felt like doing? Play it out mentally. It would be complete and utter chaos. You think zombies are bad? Imagine billions of people whose only criteria for decision making were their feelings and emotions and desires. It would be like shopping on Black Friday.

At the time of writing this book, I've only been sucking oxygen on this planet for thirty-eight years, so bear with me. In my limited experience, I have not met a single person who has told me, "My general philosophy in life is to do what I feel like when I feel like doing it, and it has brought me incredible happiness and fulfillment and peace. I just follow every fleeting feeling. That is how I live my life, and it's the secret to my happiness."

I have never met that person.

What I have found instead is that fulfillment, peace, joy,

and health on the inside are, ironically, often found by doing the exact opposite of what we feel like doing in the moment.

Let me clarify: I'm not advocating an emotionless life. That would be both impossible and boring. Nor am I saying our emotions can't color and shape our decisions either, because they should and they do. And I'm a huge fan of spontaneity and living in the moment.

But as I said earlier, our feelings don't rule our lives. That is why we must question them. It is helpful, healthy, and humbling to admit that maybe what we feel is flat-out wrong.

The second thing that stands out in these two psalms is the answer the songwriter gives us: "Hope in God."

It's a simple statement, but keep the context in mind. The author is lost, confused, and hopeless. So he looks at his options, and he comes to this conclusion: *Either life is meaningless and my existence doesn't matter—or God is the only hope I have.*

When we consider the magnitude and proliferation of pain and suffering on this planet, those are really the only two conclusions we can come to. On one hand, maybe God isn't real and life is an accident. If that is true, then our lives have no significance beyond the present. Our existence is a quirk and a coincidence. There is no right or wrong. Someday we will cease to exist. We will pass into oblivion and none of this will have mattered.

But on the other hand, maybe there is a God. Maybe there is a rhyme and a reason to our existence. Maybe we are here because a creator, an architect, a being bigger than us is actively at work in the universe. If that is true, it stands to reason that he would reveal himself to us. Not only that, but he would be committed to preserving and protecting and loving his creation.

Therefore, when we find ourselves tumbling down melancholy rabbit holes of discouragement and depression, we have to choose. Either we believe that nothing matters, or we put our hope in someone who is bigger than us—God.

I think this mental wrestling match is exactly what is happening in these two psalms. We are witnessing the inner turmoil of someone who is facing his options. And he chooses hope. He chooses to turn to God, and that makes all the difference.

Notice that the artist has a history with God. He says, "Hope in God, for I shall again praise him." The word *again* means that he has praised him in the past, back before life got confusing and his soul slipped out of alignment. Things might be terrible now, but there was a day where he had seen and proven God's goodness.

That memory gives him the hope he needs. So instead of allowing his thoughts to stay mired in the quicksand of his emotions, he looks at the future. If he could trust God in the past, he can trust him for the future. He might be surprised by his soul right now, but he's not subject to his soul. He is not trapped by his feelings forever.

He says, *My life feels upside down right now, but I'm going to fix my gaze on God. I'm going to put my hope in him. I know him, and he's going to work this thing out. Yes, these feelings are confusing, but they are going to fade, and I will praise God again.*

Chances are you've seen God's hand at work in your life. Maybe you didn't recognize it for what it was. Maybe it was hard to believe that God could be found anywhere in what you were going through. But later you looked back and realized that even in dark times, God was right there with you.

Take time to think about those experiences. Remember God's goodness, presence, and power. Your feelings come and go, but God remains the same, and you will praise him again. It's only a matter of time.

The songwriter goes on. He says, "Hope in God, for I shall again praise him, my salvation and my God."

That is interesting language. *My* salvation. *My* God.

A lot of people believe in *a* God. That's within reason. That's logical. But the artist calls him *his* salvation and *his* God. In other words, God isn't just an impersonal, distant, unfeeling boss of the universe. He is personal. He is present. He is with us and he is for us even when we can't see past our problems.

I am convinced that an awareness of God's care for us is the key to emotional sanity. Life is too big, too unknown, and too confusing for us to figure it out on our own. Many people think that whatever happens to them is up to them, that they are the navigators and controllers of their destiny. That's great when life is smooth—but ultimately it is a self-defeating approach, because when they most need help, they have no one to turn to.

God is *our* God. He is *our* salvation. His full attention is toward us. It is hard for our finite selves to fathom that the most powerful person in the universe could be intimately involved in our everyday lives, but it's true. And this reality and knowledge and awareness will rescue us from the cycle of despair.

No one else in the universe can be our hope, by the way.

Your best friend can't save you. Your spouse will let you down. Your pastor is just as human as you are.

One of the occupational hazards of pastoring is that sometimes people want me to be their hope and their salvation. That's scary, because it's impossible. I can't save anyone—I need a savior myself.

Someone will say something like, "Man, I thought we were friends, but sometimes you just aren't there for me. The other day I needed help with my marriage. But you didn't call me. You didn't text me back. You started to, because I saw those little blue bubbles on my phone, but then they disappeared. Why didn't you help me, Judah?"

And inside I'm thinking, *The reason I didn't text you back when you asked for marriage counseling was because when you wrote me, I was actually in the middle of a fight with my wife. So I wasn't really in the mood to hand out advice.*

Maybe we don't trust in others, but we trust in ourselves. We think, *I'm going to try harder. I'm going to be better. I'm going to pick myself up out of this pit.* But sooner or later, we realize we can't be our own hope. We can't save ourselves.

That is why the artist says, "Hope in God." Not other people. Not ourselves. Not knowledge. Not hard work. Not rules or religion. Not good intentions or good works or good luck.

Please understand what I'm saying. Those things are admirable. But they won't make you whole on the inside. The God who created the universe is constantly concerned and involved in your life. That is the most emotionally stabilizing force that could ever exist.

God is not just the God of the universe. He is your God, your salvation, and your hope. He is available to you. His attention and care are perpetually toward you. They will never be removed from you. You can talk to him. You can involve him. He knows your feelings and emotions better than you do. He knows what you are going through. He knows your ups and he knows your downs.

The reality of God's care for you makes you healthy on the inside. It enables you to rise again, to believe again, and to walk again.

His care and concern do not depend on your performance, by the way. Remember, it wasn't your idea to ask for God to look out for you—he promised to do so long before you were even born. The Bible is full of God's promises to guide your steps and keep your soul. You can approach him with confidence no matter where you find yourself, because he cares for you more than you could ever deserve or describe.

Yes, life is complicated and unpredictable. You can't always explain—much less control—the emotions and feelings that wash over you from time to time. When your emotions surprise you and your feelings betray you, you need a source of hope greater than your soul. You need an anchor for your soul. And as we'll see in the next chapter, God has already provided that anchor. It's not a concept, a philosophy, or an ideology.

It's a person. And his name is Jesus.

four

AN ANCHOR FOR MY SOUL

Recently someone asked me, "Are you nautical?"

I was like, "Well, back in the eighties or nineties I had some of that clothing, for sure . . ."

The person wasn't tracking with me. "No, I mean are you good with boats and stuff?"

I said, "Absolutely not. Why would you even ask?"

"Because you are from Seattle."

He obviously didn't know me well, because I'm not a handy person. I don't really do manual things well. Basically I'm great at talking—and nothing else. Chelsea and I were talking with another couple a while back, and I think the man was under a bit of duress from his wife that he wasn't doing enough around the house, so he started listing out all the things he does. "I do the finances, and I do quite a bit of cooking actually, and I vacuum sometimes. And I do the dishes—the dishes are my deal."

We were supposed to be helping them work through their

marriage issues, but I was starting to sweat because I've never done any of those things. I looked at Chelsea for support. "Babe, what do I do?"

She replied, "You don't do anything."

That stung. I was like, "Really? I gave you three kids. And I can give you more if you want."

On a recent vacation, I took it upon myself to empty the dishwasher. I won't load it—ever—because those dishes are used and dirty and have food particles encrusted on them. But I decided I could at least deal with clean dishes. When I was done, I started telling everyone about it. I was looking for affirmation or something.

My son walked by, and I said, "Hey, Zion, check it out."

"What?"

"I unloaded the dishwasher." I could tell he wasn't impressed. "Man, it was *packed*. We're going through a lot of dishes here on vacation."

"Seriously, Dad?" And he kept walking.

Inside I thought, *Boy, I brought you into this world and I can take you out.* Anyway, that was a huge baby step for me.

All of that is just to illustrate how *not* handy or outdoorsy I am, so I'm definitely not nautical. That makes the following story completely unexplainable. But it happened.

A few summers ago, Elijah and Annemarie, who are two of our best friends, and Chelsea and I decided to get a boat and sail the ocean blue. I think it may have been my idea. It was not one of my better ones, in retrospect, because none of my fellow sailors were nautical either.

Annemarie found a used boat online. It was old but barely used, the lady said. And it only cost three hundred dollars, which was perfect. We went over to the lady's house to get it. It was actually a rowboat, I found out later, but at the time I didn't see the rowers or oars or whatever they are called, so I didn't realize that. I talked her down fifty bucks. This deal was getting sweeter by the minute. We paid her, and for some reason she looked at us like we were idiots or tourists or something.

The max weight of the boat was 380 pounds. That was unfortunate because I'm 178 when I'm working out, and Elijah is somewhere around that as well. Our wives weigh like 95 pounds each. But it didn't matter because this thing had *cup holders*. Such a good deal.

Next we found a vintage motor, which just means it was really old. Older than me, actually. But according to the seller, it also was barely used. I'm a sucker for that kind of marketing. *Barely used? Vintage? I'll take it.*

Now we were ready to sail Puget Sound. We were determined to embrace our Seattle heritage and become nautical people, at least for an afternoon.

We got the boat in the water next to the shore. We still hadn't latched on the motor yet, because we couldn't figure out how.

Unknown to us, a barge had planned to come by at that precise moment. I didn't know about wakes, but I learned quickly because a few seconds after the barge sailed past, the waves started rolling in and the boat filled up with water.

In case you are unfamiliar with Puget Sound, it looks like a lake, but it's actually the *ocean*. I don't think I really understood that before. But I was starting to figure it out.

When the tsunamis rolled in, Elijah and I were in the water trying to pretend we were handy enough to attach a motor to a rowboat. Then we saw the boat capsizing, and we panicked. So we did what any brawny, manly sailor would do: we yelled for our wives to help. "Chelsea, Annemarie, it's sinking! Get the boat! That's why we married you." So they pulled the boat up on shore and tipped it over—what kind of husbands are we?—to drain the water.

Then we flipped it back over, pushed off from shore a bit, and all climbed in. Somehow we attached the motor and then fully pushed out from shore. There we were, four grown adults in one poor rowboat with a little motor jerry-rigged to the back. We all had cups of ice water. Why? Because there were cup holders. It was meant to be.

We started up the motor. I expected to hear a satisfying roar, the sound of a robust engine capable of braving ocean currents and keeping us out of the way of wakes and waves and whales. Instead, at full throttle, all we got was a high-pitched buzzing sound that sounded more like a band of drunken mosquitoes. I'm sure I could snore louder than that motor.

At this point our boat was exactly four inches out of the water. You think I am exaggerating, but I'm not. I do that sometimes, but not right now. We were four inches from total tragedy. Four inches from reenacting the story of Jonah. There really are whales in Puget Sound, folks. And seals and sea lions and probably sharks.

At first I was a little unsettled, but I tried to convince myself it was okay. "This is awesome, isn't it, Elijah?"

"Yeah, it's amazing! I'm loving it."

And inside we were all thinking, *This is not going to end well.*

Another barge came rolling through town. By this time we were six hundred-plus yards off shore, at least.

I was telling this story to someone, and he interrupted me at this point. "Can't you swim?"

I was like, "Yeah, but I don't want to! What kind of question is that? I live on land."

Anyway, the barge barged through, as barges do, and waves started pummeling us. I was shocked by certain passengers' reactions to this. There were pastors on board who might have used some explicit words, and I was totally disappointed. I started talking to God, but they were saying all kinds of stuff. I was thinking, *I can't believe I even married you!* Just kidding. Maybe.

The boat again started filling with water, only now we were out too far to make our wives save us. We started using the cups that we had intended to drink out of to bail water out of our boat. I was thinking, *This is not right. This is not how I saw this going down. Wait—are we going to die?*

We didn't die, obviously. We spent the next four hours weaving and bobbing and dodging barges to a sound track of drunken mosquitoes. We were living the dream on a rowboat with a 1976 motor, four inches from every man for himself.

Have you ever felt four inches from disaster? Maybe you were emotionally, internally, mentally, or even spiritually four inches from giving up. Four inches from being completely submerged.

Four inches from tragedy, from calamity, from saying, *I'm done. I can't handle this anymore. This is too much.*

It's not just bad things that can get you to this place, by the way. Sometimes success can take you there. The things you dreamed of, the things you worked for, the things you were passionate about—when you finally achieve that income or prominence or position you imagined, you find that it has brought you four inches from being overwhelmed.

If you can't relate to that feeling of impending disaster—whether it's the result of too many painful things or too many good things or a combination of both—then you must be about six years old. Because for all of us normal humans living on this painful, fragmented, broken planet, this is life.

I'm sure you know the feeling. We have all lived long enough to experience this once or twice or a hundred times. *If one more barge sails by, if one more unexpected thing happens, if I get one more bit of bad news, I'm going to sink internally and emotionally. I'm going to call it quits.*

As I write this chapter, news of another incomprehensible terrorist attack targeting civilians is flooding the media channels, and my heart is breaking yet again. There seems to be a constant stream of tragedy upon atrocity upon calamity in this world. I can't process it. I can't reconcile it. I can't understand it. We are living in unsettled, uncertain times.

This world can be so pained and so difficult, and in almost an instant our souls can go from being buoyant to being four inches from capsizing.

A BETTER ANCHOR

In the previous chapter we talked about the surprising emotions of our souls and about how God is our souls' source of hope. Now I want to look in more detail at how God is our souls' source of stability. I am convinced that our inner needs for security, strength, and solidity can be met only when our souls find their homes in God.

Hebrews 6:17–20 describes this reality:

> So when God desired to show more convincingly to the heirs of the promise the unchangeable character of his purpose, he guaranteed it with an oath, so that by two unchangeable things, in which it is impossible for God to lie, we who have fled for refuge might have strong encouragement to hold fast to the hope set before us. We have this as a sure and steadfast anchor of the soul, a hope that enters into the inner place behind the curtain, where Jesus has gone as a forerunner on our behalf, having become a high priest forever after the order of Melchizedek.

This particular passage was written to Jewish people two thousand years ago, so it has historical and cultural references that might not immediately resonate today. But when you take a closer look, you realize God is speaking to us about an innate need that is as universal as it is timeless: the need for stability.

I read these verses recently and asked myself a simple

question: Does my soul have an anchor? Because evidently my soul needs one—that's the point of this passage.

Remember, we are defining the soul as the "inside you." It's your heart; your inner being; your mind, will, and emotions. If you are like me, your soul has a tendency to drift like a boat on a sea. The purpose of an anchor is to keep you from drifting. It keeps you from being carried by every wake and current that swirls past. Ultimately, it keeps you from capsizing.

In retrospect, our rowboat could have used an anchor. And a real motor. And a better crew, for that matter. But hey—we had cup holders.

An anchor is an agent of stability. It is an agent of security. It is an agent of steadiness. You tether yourself to it, and no matter how unpredictable or challenging the elements become, you remain stable.

There is a reason we find this passage in a letter to the early Jewish Jesus followers. It was written to people who heard and believed that their long-awaited Messiah, their Savior, had indeed come, and his name was Jesus Christ of Nazareth.

The moment these Hebrews believed in Jesus, their lives dramatically changed. Because of religious persecution, many of them lost family members, friends, businesses, and jobs. They were hurting. They were suffering economically, financially, emotionally, and physically because they had decided to follow Jesus.

The author of Hebrews wrote to two main groups of people. The first group was composed of people who were four inches from giving up. These people were thinking, *I'm done. This is too difficult. This is too painful. Following Jesus has cost me in so many areas. I've lost friends and loved ones. Jesus isn't worth this.* So the writer told them, "Don't give up on Jesus."

The second group were those who wanted to just add Jesus to their conglomeration of spiritual concepts and ideas. They wanted to believe in Jesus, but they also wanted to keep the Law and the Ten Commandments. They had a hybrid spirituality that tried to mesh faith in Jesus with other spiritual paths. The author wrote to tell them, "Jesus is enough."

Hebrews uses seafaring imagery to refer to Jesus. I am qualified to explain this, in case you were wondering, because I am nautical now. Four hours of experience makes all the difference.

That brings us to our passage in Hebrews 6. The author used the familiar imagery of a boat and an anchor to remind these ancient Jesus followers that when they felt overwhelmed, they needed to hang on to Jesus. Jesus was enough for them; they just needed to hold on to the hope of their souls, regardless of the tumult and torrent around them. The writer painted a beautiful portrait of the hope and security and stability we have in Jesus. He said, "We have this as a sure and steadfast anchor of the soul."

Then he referenced the Jewish priesthood and temple, which were essential components of Israel's belief system that were incredibly rich in symbolism and metaphor. The writer was reminding these Jesus followers that the history, the miracles, the writings and prophecies, the spiritual principles and religious ceremonies they had cherished and followed for centuries—all of this ultimately pointed to Jesus. Their hope wasn't in a religious system or set of commandments, but in a person. Jesus was the immovable, eternal anchor of their souls.

We need to be reminded of the same thing. Two thousand years later, not much has changed in human nature. We still find our souls overwhelmed at times, and we still need an anchor.

When I asked myself, "Does my soul have an anchor?" that instantly triggered a related question: "*What* is my anchor?" In other words, where do I turn when I feel overwhelmed? When I feel like I am drowning inside? When I need an escape?

I've heard all kinds of answers to that question over the years. Some people say, "Well, I'm debt free. That's the key. My house is paid off. I have a plan for retirement. I have money in the bank. I'm set for life." Ultimately the anchors of their souls are their jobs, their education, their connections and prominence, or their cleverness.

I'm all for financial stability and career planning. But let's be honest—that approach has holes. Life isn't neat and tidy and controlled. It's not predictable. We prepare for the worst and hope for the best, but we are still subject to the whims and whimsy of time and chance.

The bottom line is that things that do not have souls cannot aid people who do have souls. Your car will not help you when you are discouraged. It will not sustain your soul, even though it has heated seats and GPS and a plethora of cup holders. It can't help you because it doesn't have a soul, and you do. Your house does not have a soul. Your job doesn't have a soul. Your social prominence and position do not have souls. By definition and by nature, these things do not have the ability within themselves to aid you in your mind, your will, or your emotions.

Some people might answer this question by saying, "My anchor is my man. He is godly, he is strong, he is brave." Or maybe, "My anchor is my girl. She is beautiful. We are perfect together. We can conquer anything." Someone else might say, "I'm a family guy. My anchor is my kids, my grandkids, my family. Nothing can separate us. We are here for each other no matter what." Some people anchor themselves in their friends. "We are BFFs. We've been through hell and high water. As long as I have him or her in my life, I'm good."

Yes, people have souls. So this answer is definitely a step up from tethering your security to your 401(k) or that property you bought on the lake. I'm all for friends and family. Natural family, spiritual family, church family, friends close by and friends far away—our relationships really do make a difference.

But even this answer has holes in it, because that person you are counting on has a soul that is just as fragile and fragmented as yours and mine. He or she will be there for you sometimes, but not all the time.

Many people go into marriage thinking that their spouses will be their source of stability. But they end up hurt and frustrated because they let each other down. So they complain, "You're never there for me." And the instant reply is, "Well, you aren't there for me either." It turns into an old-fashioned Western standoff where neither party will lower their gun first. "Well, I feel like you just don't care. And you don't listen to me. You don't meet my needs or my expectations. I'm not happy and I'm not sure I even love you anymore."

The problem isn't lack of love. It's impossible expectations.

It's the belief that our souls can find ultimate satisfaction and strength by anchoring themselves to another human soul. But person after person lets us down because their souls are hurting too. We tie ourselves to each other, then we both end up nearly drowned by the storms of life.

We squabble and complain, "Why haven't you saved me yet?"

And the other yells back, "I don't know! I thought you were going to help me!"

The problem is, we can't save each other. We can't anchor each other. So what is the solution?

We need somebody with a soul. It needs to be a soul similar to ours, a soul that knows our plight and condition. But at the same time, it needs to be a soul that is profoundly different, a soul that is flawless and perfect and whole. That is the only soul that can fix us, because it doesn't have to fix itself.

That's where Jesus comes in.

I'm sure you knew I was going to say that. I always end up there because I'm convinced it is true. Jesus is the anchor our souls long for.

Maybe you say, "I'm not really a Jesus guy. I'm not really into church and religious stuff."

That's okay. That's your decision to make. But let me just appeal to you for a moment. If it's not Jesus, then all I'm saying is you need to find another divine, perfect being who is completely familiar with humanity, someone who has lived among us and yet lived sinlessly and perfectly. Find a being who has a soul that is flawless but who can totally relate to our souls; someone who transcends us and yet is completely involved with us; someone who is intimately aware of our fragility and depravity but yet is unconditionally and unswervingly in love with us; someone who can rescue us and save us in every high and low of life. All I'm saying is, if not Jesus, just find someone a lot like him.

HELICOPTER JESUS

Jesus is the sure and steadfast anchor of our souls. But to be honest, I wish the writer of Hebrews hadn't said *anchor*. I read this and thought, *I wish it said helicopter of my soul.*

When I'm in a storm, I'd much rather have a helicopter than an anchor. An anchor implies that I am going to stay right where I am. But I'd like to escape, actually. I'd like a helicopter with some well-trained Navy SEALS on board who can hoist me up and fly me away from my reality.

People sign up for helicopter Jesus all the time. *I cannot wait to follow Jesus,* they think, *because he's my heavenly helicopter. Get me out, Father! Hoist away, Jesus! Beam me up, Scotty!*

I think I just inserted Star Trek into the Trinity. Sorry about that.

Storms hit, and we say, "Jesus, I don't want to stay here. I don't like this at all. It's windy. It's rainy. The waves are big. Where is my heavenly helicopter?"

And Jesus replies, "I'll be your anchor."

We want out. We want an escape. We want someone to remove us from the storm, but Jesus wants to be our strength and stability *in* the storm.

The Gospels record a couple of different incidents involving Jesus, the disciples, and boats caught in storms. One of these is found in Matthew 14. Jesus tells his disciples to get in a boat and cross the Sea of Galilee. Not as impressive as Puget Sound, but still a big deal.

"Where are you going?" they ask.

"To climb a mountain. And pray. I'll meet you on the other side."

"Wait—how are you getting there?"

"Don't worry about it. Bye."

So they start rowing, and everything goes wrong. Night falls, the wind is blowing so hard they can't get anywhere, and the waves are starting to scare even these seasoned fishermen. At this point, what do they want?

They want a helicopter.

Actually, I'm pretty sure they didn't think exactly that, since this was a couple of millennia before humans figured out how to fly. But you get the point. They want *out*. They want to be on the other side, but they can't seem to make any headway.

Then Jesus comes strolling out to meet them. This is the same Jesus who can calm the wind and the waves. But he doesn't. Instead, he scares them nearly to death because they think he's a ghost.

Jesus says, "Calm down, everyone. It's me."

I told Chelsea to calm down once, and it almost ended up being the last thing I ever said. So I can't imagine Jesus' statement being particularly reassuring for these poor guys. It's about three in the morning, they are cold and wet, and now Jesus is going all Ghostbusters on them. Apparently he has a sense of humor.

Peter says, "If it's really you, tell me to come to you."

Think about the logic behind that. Frankly, there is none. I have no idea what Peter was thinking. If it wasn't Jesus, this was not going to end well.

Jesus says, "Come."

People say all the time that Peter walked on water. That's not entirely accurate. He walked on *waves*. That's taking water-walking to another level. I read this and think, *Jesus, why the waves? It would be impressive enough if he walked on normal smooth water. Why do you have to make it even harder?*

You have to give Peter credit. He takes a few steps. But then he sees the wind and waves and starts to sink. It reminds me of those Road Runner cartoons they had when I was a kid where the characters always ran off cliffs but never actually fell until they looked down. I always wanted to yell at the screen, "Don't look down! Just turn around and walk back slowly!"

Peter looks down. He starts to sink. Jesus reaches out and grabs him. Then he has the gall, the nerve, and the audacity to call Peter out. "Peter, bro—why did you doubt? Why so little faith?"

If I were Peter, I'd be like, "Uh, why am I doubting? Are you serious right now, Jesus? I'll stop doubting when you turn off the wind machine."

Do you ever read the Bible like that? With actual emotion and normal human responses? Sometimes we read these stories and we make them so picturesque and Renaissance. I'm sure Peter at that moment did not feel like a saintly figure in a medieval painting. He was cold, wet, terrified, and intensely human. And Jesus says, "Why did you doubt?"

If we're honest, we've all had moments like that. We read scriptures that encourage us to trust in God and they sound great on paper, but then we look around and we get overwhelmed. *I'll tell you exactly why I'm doubting,* we think. *Have you seen the wind? The waves? Did you hear the diagnosis from my doctor? Do you read the news? How can I not doubt? I'm sinking right now, and I have no idea what to do.*

Jesus is saying something with this question. By the way, he is *always* saying something when he asks a question. Jesus' questions are absolutely rhetorical. They are sneaky statements designed to help us reflect and learn.

Jesus doesn't want Peter to list out the reasons he panicked. "Well, Jesus, since you asked, here are the four things that are freaking me out right now . . ."

That's not what he is saying. He is reminding Peter, "You really have no reason to doubt, because I am here. I am with you. I am caring for you. I am your anchor and your rock and your God."

In the middle of our storms and waves, God asks us the same thing. *Why do you doubt?* He's not asking that in order to condemn us or mock us, but to remind us that we really have no reason to doubt. Jesus is with us.

Before you get too hard on yourself for not trusting God at times, consider this. The physical, tangible, visible Jesus was right in front of Peter, and Peter still had trouble keeping his eyes on Jesus because the waves were so big.

We don't have that luxury. Jesus isn't physically here. When you lost your job, Jesus didn't appear in his robe and sandals and well-groomed beard to say, "Here, let me help you pack up your cardboard box." It doesn't happen that way, does it? We are asked to trust in a Jesus we can't see.

But here's the thing about anchors. An anchor does its best work where it is never seen. An anchor plunges through the depths of the sea until it settles and wedges itself into the ocean floor. Meanwhile, back on the surface, in the boat that is your soul, you continue to be buffeted by the elements of life. All you can see in the moment are the wind and waves. But under the surface, you have an anchor.

Jesus asks us all: "Why do you doubt? The anchor is set. The work is finished. My love is for you and toward you. I am near. I will care for you in this life and the life to come."

Notice that Jesus asks Peter this question while they are still hovering above the depths. They aren't in the boat yet. The wind and waves are bigger than ever. Jesus wasn't being mean to Peter. He wanted him to think about his reaction. Peter needed to realize that Jesus is just as trustworthy in the storm as in the calm.

The parallel to our lives is clear. It's easy to have faith when we are safely in the boat—when the wind is gone and the stars are out. But can we trust Jesus in the midst of the storm? Because that is when we need him the most.

To conclude the story, let me point out one more thing. The apostle John recorded this same story, and he mentioned an interesting detail. He said that when Jesus got into the boat, "immediately the boat was at the land to which they were going" (John 6:21).

That's just like Jesus. One moment you are in a storm and you are terrified and confused and alone. But then suddenly, somehow, you are where you wanted to be. You hardly know how you got there. There was a time not too long before when you thought you'd never make it, that the storms and waves were going to win. But you held on, and God got you through.

People come up to you and say, "You are an overnight success! You are so lucky. Everything just works out for you."

And you're like, "You have no idea . . ."

I've noticed that God often takes us from point A to point B in a way that is simultaneously exhilarating and nerve-wracking. Not because he wants to torment us, but because he wants us to realize that the point is not really crossing the lake—the point is simply being with Jesus. It is living our lives from a place of trust and rest that comes when we truly know him.

Do you feel a bit overwhelmed right now? Are you four inches from drowning? Are you fending off crazy, bizarre feelings and ideas? *I'm going to leave, I'm going to run, I'm going to be done. I can't do this anymore.*

Tether yourself again to the only true security in life, the only true anchor: Jesus. I can't promise you that the wind will instantly cease or the waves will immediately calm. But I can promise you that he will keep you safe in the midst of the storm. He is everything you need. And when you get through the storm, you will find yourself in a place of stability, faith, and fruitfulness that can come only from him.

Whatever you do, don't give up. You have a sure and steadfast anchor of the soul, and he will see you safely to the other side.

five

IS LOVE GOD OR
IS GOD LOVE?

I was called out recently on my habit of overusing the word *love*. I'll be the first to admit that this person was right. But I doubt I'll change, because I am a romantic at heart. I love the word *love*. I love the concept of love. I love to love and be loved. I love to tell everyone, "I love you." I am indiscriminate and outspoken in my declarations of love.

I really mean it when I tell people I love them. The problem is that my affection and endearment also extend to inanimate objects. "I love my outfit today." "I love that paint color." "Oh my gosh, I love SportsCenter." *Love* is a word that just makes sense to me.

Anyway, the person who mentioned my tendency to overuse the word *love* actually caught me expressing my undying love to my children and corn nuts in the same sentence.

I know we are all in a health craze right now, so maybe you've tried to forget corn nuts. These days we pay twenty-two dollars for lunch because it has kale, and we ask for it with almond milk. That's society now. But before we milked almonds, there were corn nuts. I used to have them when I was in grade school. Corn nuts were amazing.

A lot of people gave up on corn nuts because they put them in the same category as Captain Crunch, but that is a great error. Corn nuts were a health food before we were aware that we should have health food. Have you ever seen the ingredients? Corn, oil, salt. It's a healthy snack. So lately I've been obsessed with corn nuts. I'll go to Safeway and get five large bags of corn nuts. Not only are corn nuts delicious and healthy, they are consistent—every corn nut is just as salty and crunchy and satisfying as the last. How could you not love corn nuts?

I think my sentence went something like this. "Oh my gosh, I love my kids, because they are just the best, and hey, lately I just can't get enough of these corn nuts, because I really love them. So crunchy and salty and always amazing. I forgot about corn nuts. Have you tried them recently?"

My friend said, "Are you serious?"

"Yeah, they are salty, crunchy . . ."

"No, no. I mean you just said that you love your kids and you love corn nuts in the same sentence. You have a problem."

I wanted to punch him. But he was right.

Eighteen years ago Chelsea and I were on our second date. We were at Applebee's. I made a reservation because it gets busy at Applebee's on Friday nights. We had ordered some exquisite Applebee's cuisine, like hot wings or something.

I had told myself that I was not going to say "I love you" to Chelsea until I knew we were going to get married. We've known each other our entire lives, and back in middle school I told her I loved her all the time. I was trying to reel things back in and recover my innocence, so I committed to myself that I wasn't going to tell her I loved her until things were much more serious.

But Applebee's always wins. The atmosphere is irresistible. There we were, day two of dating, and I leaned back after the meal and sighed without really thinking, "Oh my word, I love you."

She was like, "Excuse me?"

I stuttered, "No, no! Nothing!"

"What, you don't love me?"

"No—I mean—just forget that I said anything."

Six months later, we were at my sister's wedding. We were in the wedding party, so we were walking down the aisle together. It was so romantic, and I decided it was the moment to finally declare my feelings. I turned and whispered dramatically in her ear, "Chelsea, I love you."

She didn't miss a step as she whispered back, "You already said that at Applebee's."

I'm not the only one who overuses the word *love*, though. It's a common habit in our society and culture today. We are obsessed with love. Love is what life is all about, it seems. We love romantic movies and candlelit dinners. We love smells, we love cars, we love toothpaste, we love shoes, we love feelings, we love fresh flowers. Our souls yearn and search and long to *love*.

Maybe that is why the definition of love has gotten a little bit lost in the mix. Love might be the single greatest need of the human soul, but if we are honest, we are not entirely sure what it is. Is it chemistry? Emotion? Commitment? Self-sacrifice? Lust? Passion? Instinct? A choice? A philosophy? A myth?

In case you were wondering, I won't be resolving millennia of philosophical and poetic ponderings in this chapter. But I want to look at what I think is the key to understanding and experiencing love.

LOVE IS GOD?

That key, simply put, is the realization that God is love. It is knowing, believing, and living in the love of God. It is experiencing God's love for us on a soul level, and as a result learning to love as he loves. The apostle John wrote:

> Beloved, let us love one another, for love is from God, and whoever loves has been born of God and knows God. Anyone who does not love does not know God, because God is love. In this the love of God was made manifest among us, that God sent his only Son into the world, so that we might live through him. (1 John 4:7–9)

God is love, and God designed our souls to thrive within the context of authentic love. Just like our need for hope and our need for stability, which we looked at in the previous chapters, love is a fundamental desire of our souls. We naturally seek to be loved and to love. Our souls find security and happiness and identity in this concept called love. And while that looks different for different people, ultimately our souls cannot be at home without love.

God is the original lover. He is the perfect, consistent, all-encompassing personification of love. He defines love and he is the source of love. He is the one who created the concept of love and the one who introduced us to love. Love and God are meant to go together.

The problem is that people who claim to know God have not always been the greatest representation of God's love to humanity. Some people who say they represent God or act in the name of Jesus have done horrible, deplorable things. And it's not all in the past either. Our world is being rocked right now by atrocities committed in the name of God and religion.

On a less violent but more widespread level, many people who claim that God is love are also outspoken in their judgment and criticism toward those who don't agree with them or who don't live up to their standards. And while some of their accusations and rebukes might have a basis in truth, their approach comes across as hateful and often hypocritical.

Partly as a result of these misrepresentations of God's love, many people choose to disassociate human love and divine love. It makes sense if you think about it. So rather than saying that God is love, the logic goes, let's take the divine, abusive, mean, rigid, exclusive, judgmental elements out of love, and just make *love* God. Love is God, man. Let's just love each other. Make love, not war. Everyone love each other, be cool, smoke the herbs of the earth, and wear tie-dye. Hashtag Woodstock. God? Jesus? Bible? Organized religion? No, love is what's important, because love is God.

Initially, it's incredibly alluring to say love is God: to make life about love, to put our hope in love, and to elevate love above all else. If everyone would just love each other, imagine what this planet would look like. It sounds amazing. Love would conquer hate and violence and war. Love would meet the needs of the poor and help those affected by tragedies. It would regulate injustice and share the resources of the world with everyone. Love should work . . . right?

Except it hasn't. Despite our world's fixation with love; despite the peace movement and the civil rights movement; despite thousands of poems, songs, movies, books, and speeches about love, we still find ourselves surrounded by an inordinate amount of hatred.

Why does a philosophy that says "love is God" not work? Because it is inherently a disconnected philosophy. It is an ideal that defines itself by itself. What is love? No one knows, because there is no standard or definition for love.

So let's play this logic out. Imagine a conversation with a friend who is committed to this philosophy.

You ask, "Who is God?"

And your fictional friend replies, "Love is God."

"So who is in charge?"

"Love."

"Okay, and who defines love?"

He says, "Well, love defines itself."

You reply, "Um, no, it doesn't. Love is not an intelligent entity. It can't do that."

"Well, I don't know, man, I just think love is . . ."

"Wait, 'you think'? So are you defining love? Does that make you God?"

"I don't know. It's weird that you would say it like that."

"Well, you are defining love. So that makes you in charge."

"Well, not me—just like, my friends."

"Okay, so you and your friends are God?"

You've got to love imaginary conversations, right? You win the argument every time.

Here's the problem. If love is God but we all get to make up our own definitions of love, then ultimately we all are God. Because when you replace a person with a concept, whoever defines that concept has ultimate authority.

If you say that the ruling, defining, ultimate standard for the universe is love, it sort of begs the whole "What is love?" question. Love can't make decisions, so humans like you and me end up doing our best to understand and enforce what love is supposed to look like. According to us, anyway.

Confused? That's my point. A universe ruled by self-appointed lexicographers of love would be chaos. Everybody doing love by his or her own definition would be pure pandemonium.

When you remove human love from divine love, you are left with lawlessness. You don't want to be part of an economy where love is God. You don't want to be part of an education system where love is God. You don't want to have a weekend getaway in a place where love is God. Love without God produces an abstract society where everyone is their own god, and they live by their own impulses and their own feelings. "This is love to me, so I'm going to do it."

And their kids or spouses or neighbors reply, "This isn't love—this is abuse. This is horrible. This is wicked."

"No, this is love. This is right. You have to let me do this, because this is what I think love is telling me to do."

Love is God? It sounds sexy, but eventually it leaves you displaced and lost because what is paramount remains undefined.

What I am presenting to you is an appeal for better living, for a better society, and for a better culture. It is better for us to have love defined by a definitive divine being. It makes for better marriages, better families, better jobs, better pay.

God wants us to flourish. He wants us to enjoy our lives— and he wants those around us to enjoy theirs as well. That is why it is imperative that we not just understand how paramount love is but also define it in a healthy, God-inspired manner.

God is love. God invented love. So God gets to define love. And as we learn to live in his love, our souls will find themselves at home, at rest, and at peace.

If God's kind of love is paramount for our souls, what does that love look like? To answer that question, let's look at one of the greatest treatises ever written on the subject of divine love, 1 Corinthians 13. Here are verses 4–7:

> Love is patient and kind; love does not envy or boast; it is
> not arrogant or rude. It does not insist on its own way; it is
> not irritable or resentful; it does not rejoice at wrongdoing,

but rejoices with the truth. Love bears all things, believes all things, hopes all things, endures all things.

Paul was writing to the church at Corinth. In case you've never heard of Corinth, it was an ancient city in Greece that was basically a hybrid of Amsterdam, Las Vegas, and Hollywood, only crazier. It was a highly sexualized city, a city where love was God and sensuality was almost deified.

Meanwhile, a group of committed followers of Jesus was trying to build a community and a church in the middle of this love crisis in Corinth. Paul wrote to these believers to tell them that love is not some undefined, abstract quality. Love is not a feeling. Love is not sexual anarchy. Paul reminded them that love has been put on display by the life, death, burial, and resurrection of their Lord and Savior, Jesus.

Love is a lifestyle. Love is practical. Love is something you live and walk and talk. Love does not just make for good sermons—love makes for good living.

It's worth noting that this chapter is found in a letter known not for sentimental feelings but rather for outright rebukes. Paul wrote 1 Corinthians to the church at Corinth to correct a number of abuses he had heard about. Smack in the middle of his corrections and discipline, he took time out to remind the Corinthians about the nature of true love.

Why? Because love really does change things. Woodstock wasn't wrong about that. But the only kind of love that can create the change we need is the love of God—a love motivated by, empowered by, and defined by God. God inspired Paul to write these words because a lot of the abuses and misunderstanding that permeated the church at Corinth would take care of themselves if people could learn to live in God's love.

Here is verse 7 again: "Love bears all things, believes all things, hopes all things, endures all things." Notice the emphasis here: *all*. In other words, there are no exceptions. There are no trapdoors, back doors, or escape hatches from love. If we are going to truly love each other like God loves us and created us to love, then we have to be committed.

It's easy to love those who love you. That's what Jesus told his disciples in his famous Sermon on the Mount (Matthew 5:43–47). But it takes a divine love, a supernatural love, to love those who do not love us back. Yet that's the only kind of love that will change the world. And it's the only kind of love that will bring lasting satisfaction and health to our souls.

Paul says that *all* the time and in *every* situation, love does these four things: bears, believes, hopes, and endures. That's the explanation and definition of love that 1 Corinthians 13:7 gives us. Let's look briefly at each of these four characteristics.

ROOFS WITHOUT SKYLIGHTS

The first term is *bear*. This letter was originally written in Greek, and the term translated *bear* is related to the Greek word for roof.[1] The term literally means "put a roof on." Figuratively, it has the idea of covering or keeping something confidential; it can also mean to put up with something.

Paul was telling the Corinthian believers that love is a roof and a cover. Love protects, shields, and conceals the weaknesses of others. The apostle Peter wrote, "Above all, keep loving one another earnestly, since love covers a multitude of sins" (1 Peter 4:8). This doesn't mean we ignore sin; it means we don't use people's faults and failures to expose or shame them. We publicly cover them and privately restore them with the goal of bringing about health in their lives.

Some people are roofs, but they have a lot of skylights. Maybe you've met people like this, or maybe you've done this yourself. I definitely have. People with skylights say things like, "Oh yeah, the Jones family, they are great. They are amazing. But their daughter Julie, you know—we love her, too, but she has a couple of issues. We're praying for her. There was that Fourth of July picnic. You didn't hear about that? She was kind of out of control. I don't mean to gossip, but she said this and did that . . . but we love her and pray for her. Oh yeah, and there was that one time . . ."

These skylight Christians have good hearts, but they are exposers, not coverers. They build skylights into every conversation because somehow the fact that they have the scoop makes them feel better about themselves.

We don't have to do that, though. We can be so secure in God's love and our identity that we don't have to give people glimpses into other people's business. We can be a safe place for hurting people, a place where they can find unconditional love and support—both public and private—while they get back on their feet.

It's interesting. We want to be able to have a few skylights ourselves, but we want to marry someone who is a solid roof. We want kids who are solid roofs. We want best friends who are solid roofs.

The Bible says here that love bears all. It covers and protects and keeps confidential everything entrusted to it. Again, we aren't talking about keeping secrets here. There is a time and place to take certain things to higher authorities or to call attention to issues that are creating danger. Rather, we are talking about shielding those who confide in us from the kind of public scrutiny and ridicule that will only harm them. We are talking about believing in people so much that we help them bear their failures and cover their weaknesses until they can be healed.

All of us are works in progress. All of us have a few faults and failures. And all of us at some point have—or wish we had—people in our lives who are solid roofs. We can be that person for someone else in our lives. That's what love does.

HE DIDN'T MEAN IT

The second word is *believe*. Love believes all things. In other words, love looks for the best. It doesn't mean you don't see the worst; it just means that even in the middle of the worst time of someone's life, you remember the best, celebrate the best, remind that person of the best, and believe the best.

This definition, "love believes all things," can be summed up in one phrase that you should insert into your vocabulary and conversation on a daily basis. "He (or she) didn't mean it."

On Monday morning when your coworker throws you under the bus in front of your boss, "love believes" needs to kick in. *She didn't mean it. I know it looked like she meant it, and it sounded like she meant it, and everyone else thinks she meant it. But I choose to believe the best. She was just trying to be funny. She wasn't thinking. She had a bad morning. She hasn't had her coffee yet. She must be facing something difficult at home. She probably regrets what she said already.*

It means you decide to believe that whatever happened wasn't what the person really meant to do or say. *I know he punched me in the face. I know he kicked my dog. But he loves dogs. And I bet he is feeling sorry right now.*

Have you ever met anyone like this? It's enough to drive you crazy. You know the person just got manipulated. You know he or she just got worked over. And how does the person respond? "They didn't mean it."

Absolutely they meant it! you think. *Pull your head out of the sand!* You want to jump in and fight for that person's rights.

Where does the desire to defend ourselves and justify ourselves and protect ourselves come from? In reality, it's a lack of God-awareness. Is God God or not? Do we trust him to take care of us or not?

Ultimately we either choose to let God be God, or we take it upon ourselves to right every wrong and defend every injustice. That's impossible, though, just FYI. We aren't capable of sorting through the motivations of our *own* hearts half the time, much less those of others. And we certainly can't expect that exacting our idea of vengeance is somehow going to solve things. It doesn't work that way. Revenge just promotes more revenge. That's why *Kill Bill* and *Ocean's Eleven* and many other revenge movies have sequels. Actually, the main reason is that it makes studios a lot of money, but you get my point.

Some of us are the self-appointed guardians of our rights, privileges, dignity, and pride. We think that if we get walked all over, if we get taken advantage of, we somehow lose something. But in reality, it's the people who live their lives defending themselves and lashing out at perceived attackers who lose the most.

Think about it. Who is primarily affected if you spend your days assuming the worst?

Yeah, that coworker meant to hurt me with that comment. My wife is so manipulative. That neighbor is always mean and underhanded and subversive.

Guess what? Those people aren't going to be bothered by your bitterness. But you are.

You will spend your life in a holding pattern, looking back at the situation from every angle, trying to figure out how to get the advantage, how to get your pride back, how to prove your point. And ironically, the situations you are obsessing over are long gone. You will never get ahead by flying in circles. You will never get over something until you let it go.

The best way to let something go is to immediately and from your heart decide not to pick up the offense in the first place. "He didn't mean it." And you move on with your life. You give people the benefit of the doubt—even when there is very little doubt. You know they meant it, but you are choosing to believe the best, to believe they regret it now, to believe that's not what they wanted for their lives, to believe that they did it in ignorance or haste or pain, but they are really not that kind of people.

If you do this, your soul will be so free. Your ice cream will taste better. Your kale will have some flavor. You will have a skip in your step and a sparkle in your eye because you are not controlled by the offenses of others.

Can you imagine what our families and marriages would look like if we included this phrase in our daily vernacular? What the church would look like? What nations and politics and media and neighborhood associations and every other societal relationship would look like?

Believe all things, because that's what love does.

OFF THE TRACKS

Two definitions down, two to go. Let me warn you, this is not going to get easier. Real love—authentic God-love—is not always easy. Especially, as we said earlier, because this is how love functions *all* the time. No exceptions, no disclaimers, no prenups.

The verse goes on: "Love bears all things, believes all things, hopes all things . . ." I want to look now at the word *hope*.

What does it mean that love always hopes? It means that love holds on to eventual development. Love recognizes that where we are is not where we will always be. We are on a journey. We are works in progress.

When you see a friend who is struggling, do you take a snapshot of how he is now, caption it, and file it away as your forever definition of him? Do you label him and limit him? Because God doesn't. And God doesn't label or limit you and me either. Your friend is a work in progress. God has him on a journey. Take a video instead, because things will change. Two years from now there's a good chance he will be ahead of you in some areas, and at that point you'll be glad you stayed humble now.

For love to be love, it can't work only when people are polished and proper and generally pleasant. Love has to work with people in the rough, with people who are anything but lovable, at least on the surface. Love has to be able to say, "I know you're on a journey, but I love you right where you are. Sooner or later you're going to make progress; but in the meantime, I love you and am committed to you."

Love needs to hope because we all have a long way to go. When we say, "You're on a journey," what we're really saying is, "You are pretty much a train wreck. You are off the tracks right now, and actually you can't even find the tracks, but God is going to put your little locomotive back on the rails and get you going really soon."

Ask yourself: Aren't you glad someone believed in you back in the day? Aren't you glad someone found you off the tracks and helped you get back on?

Love hopes all things. This could save your marriage, your family, and your friendships. Just keep hoping and believing and bearing. Sooner or later love will win.

BIGGER THAN THAT

Finally, love *endures*. To endure means you don't retaliate or reject. "I'm done with you. You crossed the line, and I'm out of here." Paul was saying that love doesn't do that. Love doesn't write people off. It doesn't give people the silent treatment. It doesn't passive aggressively dig at other people. It doesn't keep a mental list of grievances until eventually it erupts.

Love is bigger than that.

The Bible isn't saying that we ignore sin or hurt or pain. It isn't saying that we never confront. There is room in here for communication, confrontation, and restoration. But even when we confront, we do so from an attitude and an expectation that our love is not going to be withdrawn no matter what happens.

Love will be tested. Life isn't perfect and neither are we. No matter how strong the bonds or how passionate the commitments, the people we love will let us down at times. They might not mean to, but they will. And sometimes the letdowns feel intensely personal.

In moments like these, God's love is the only force strong enough to endure all things. Sooner or later, good intentions burn out. Self-discipline fails. Moral obligations and education and good manners fall short. But if we are motivated and saturated with God's love, there is no limit to what we can endure. There is no breaking point, because no matter what happens, God's love is bigger.

Jesus never hit a breaking point. He never said, "You hurt me one too many times. I'll still relate to you because I have to, but I will not let you in emotionally anymore. I have drawn the line on you."

With his dying breaths on the cross, Jesus asked God to forgive his executioners. That is the ultimate in enduring love. Jesus wasn't just trying to be a good example: "I hate you all, but just so that I look spiritual, I'm going to say I forgive you." No, his prayer reveals the essence of who he is: the personification of God's unconditional love and forgiveness.

Grace has no gaps and love knows no limits. Love endures all things.

LOVE LIKE JESUS

Where do we sign up for this lifestyle of love? A love that bears all things, believes all things, hopes all things, endures all things?

First of all, let me say that you *don't* sign up by focusing on love or by just trying harder. Self-effort is noble and admirable, and it will carry you through some things; but a love birthed in self will never be strong enough for all things. We need a love that transcends human ability and experience.

We sign up for God's kind of love by focusing on the personification and definition of love—Jesus. We looked at 1 John 4:9 earlier in this chapter. It says that God made his love manifest in Jesus. If God is love, and if God manifested his love through Jesus, then the answer to our need for love is Jesus. It is to look to Jesus, spend time with Jesus, learn from Jesus, and be loved by Jesus.

The other day I got upset at one of my kids. We were in the car, and he did something that I had told him at least five times not to do. I didn't handle it right. At all.

It was one of those times when you are too tired to actually discipline your kids, so you just threaten them. "If you do that one more time . . ." And you say that again and again, escalating in emotion and volume each time. And then finally you can't take it anymore and you go all Incredible Hulk on them. It's not right, of course. The rule of thumb is that if you find yourself losing your temper with your kids, you usually should have disciplined them earlier in the process. Give yourself a time-out and come back when you are the adult again.

But I didn't do that. I snapped. I stormed out of the car, walked to the back, opened the hatch, and fumed, "Get. Out. Of. The. Car."

He whined, "I can't—my flip-flop—"

So I grabbed the flip-flop and threw it on the ground. I didn't throw my son, for the record—just his flip-flop. It is now permanently broken. I was so angry at this point. We went for a walk down the sidewalk, and I was walking ten feet in front of him. I was trying not to eat my young.

A few minutes later, after I calmed down, I was embarrassed and frustrated with my behavior. I knew in my heart that Jesus would have handled the situation differently. My wife informed me that I had a problem. Something like, "You're handsome as heck, but you are out of control." I might have made up the first half of that.

So I texted a couple of my cousins for help. They have the

same DNA as me, and I secretly hoped they had the same problem with their tempers, because then I wouldn't be so embarrassed. But of course they are both incredibly self-controlled.

As we were texting back and forth, I mentioned, "I can't imagine Jesus doing this." Maybe he threw a couple of Peter's sandals. But Jesus wouldn't treat his children this way. Jesus knew how to love everyone, all the time, no matter what.

That was a revelation to me. Bottom line, I want to be more like Jesus. I want to look like Jesus, live like Jesus, and love like Jesus. I'm tired of trying to love my own way and in my own strength. I want more of Jesus so that I can love the way he loves.

I'm a long way from 1 Corinthians 13:7. But my desire and my prayer is that my soul would find its shelter and definition and purpose in God's love. I want to know this God of love so well and walk with him so closely that his love becomes part of the fabric of my soul.

If you found a community and a church made up of people like that, a church that doesn't just preach love and then live like grizzly bears during the week, but a church that is committed to living and loving like Jesus—wouldn't you be a part of it? If you found a neighborhood like 1 Corinthians 13:7, wouldn't you move there for the rest of your days? If you found a spouse like this, wouldn't that be the person you'd want to spend your life with? Isn't that the kind of parent you'd like to be and the kind of kids you'd like to raise?

If so, then let's be those people.

six

A QUIET SOUL

Do you have anybody truly loud in your life? I don't mean someone who can just create volume on occasion; I mean a person who is always at high volume.

Chelsea has to deal with this every day of her life because I am a loud person. I think our kids have taken it to a whole new level, though. They talk loud, they laugh loud, they tease loud, they play loud. Chelsea, however, was not raised in a loud family, nor is it in her nature to be loud, so she has had to develop loudness in the interest of self-defense. In our family, it's survival of the loudest. Sometimes I wonder if I should feel bad, because everywhere we go, we are so loud. But life is better at full volume. It's a fact.

I have a couple of friends who are louder than me. They are actually two of my favorite people in the world: Pastor Jude Fouquier, my pastor since I was eight years old, and Chad Veach, who recently started a church in Los Angeles. When I am in a conversation and happen to notice either Pastor Jude or Chad approaching, I automatically rush to finish what I am saying, because I know they are going to take over the conversation as soon as they get to me. They don't mean to. It's just that their exuberance and their decibel level are slightly overwhelming for average humanoids. *Loud* is who they are, and I love them for it.

Truly loud people can't whisper. Maybe you've noticed this. Truly loud people whisper-shout. There is no volume change when they whisper; they just get breathy. You can be in the middle of a funeral, and they lean over and whisper, "Hey, man, how are you?" And even the minister turns to look, because their voice almost raised the dead.

This is very much true of Pastor Jude. Everyone calls him *Pastor* Jude, by the way. Not Jude, not Mr. Fouquier—it's Pastor Jude. It's probably listed that way on his passport. I think even his wife calls him Pastor Jude.

Pastor Jude cannot whisper. He gets breathy, but he doesn't whisper. This is one of his challenges in life. If we are in a meeting together and I try to discreetly whisper a question to him, the entire room hears his response. So now I text him, even if he's right next to me.

One month before Chelsea and I were married, Pastor Jude and I were on a six-hour direct flight from Seattle to New York. We were going to speak at a youth conference together, so we took the same flight.

Chelsea and I were both virgins when we were married. Not that you were curious, but it's part of the story. This was partly because of our commitment to God and to purity and to each other, and partly because my mom would have killed me had we done anything prior to marriage.

Anyway, in preparation for the wedding night, someone had recommended I read a book called *A Celebration of Sex*. I don't read much—which is awkward for an author to admit—but I read that book cover to cover. It is a guide to sex and marriage and sexual fulfillment. It talks in detail about how to make sex great and exciting, and it even addresses the first night.

Pastor Jude knew that. And he decided that it was time to have "the talk."

I think we were in row 38 on Delta Airlines. We didn't have any special status; there were no upgrades in our future. So we were relegated to row 38. The problem was, the plane was totally full. Pastor Jude was in the aisle seat, I was in the middle seat, and there was a random soul stuck in 38A.

We sat down and buckled up. We hadn't even taken off yet when Pastor Jude turned and whisper-shouted, "Hey, so Judah, did you read the book on sex yet?"

I was like, "Pastor Jude, are you serious? Are we doing this right now?"

I looked at the guy in 38A out of the corner of my eye, and I could tell he was wondering if he had heard what he thought he heard.

But Pastor Jude was unaware, undeterred, and uncensored. "So what did you think? If you have any questions, just ask."

I had no questions, or at least none that I wanted announced to an airplane full of strangers.

So Pastor Jude asked all the questions. "Well, what are your plans for the first night? I recommend you start with a bath. It helps."

I was like, "Pastor Jude, *stop!*"

He said, "Oh my gosh, do you think people can hear me?"

I hissed, "Even the pilot can hear you!"

I'm not lying—for six straight hours, Pastor Jude shouted his favorite tips to me in breathy tones. This really happened. You cannot make this stuff up. If you have ever flown from Seattle to New York, it is a long flight. But it is far longer when you are sitting next to Pastor Jude a month before you get married.

During the entire flight I was unable to face the human who was sharing shoulder space with me. I couldn't imagine what 38A must be experiencing. When we finally arrived in New York, the poor man was sweating profusely. For six hours, he had not moved. He had not gone to the restroom. He had been trapped. That unsuspecting soul was inundated with more information than he ever bargained for.

TOO LOUD, TOO FAST

But that poor soul isn't the only one to get an unwanted earful. Have you noticed that we live in a loud culture? We are inundated by noise, by activity, by information. Maybe you aren't sitting in 38A next to Pastor Jude, but you are still subject to a nonstop barrage of mental and emotional stimuli.

I am trying to raise three children, and sometimes I just want to put earmuffs on them, dress them in burlap, move to

Handwritten margin notes: adjectives? adverbs? adverbs? what kind? — mom — sister — wife } roles } nouns

Montana, and live in a tree fort. They hear things and see things that I wish I could block out.

Not only is life *loud*, but it's *fast*. Our world and culture travel at a high velocity. There is so much going on, so much to hear and process. It seems we are all in a rush now.

We talk about slowing down, about shutting out the noise, about finding time to relax and decompress. That's great in theory, but I'm not sure we can control the volume and velocity of our existence, at least not completely. It's the world we live in.

Living life with this level of intensity can produce extraordinary internal angst. It can create anxiety, fear, and an overall sense of desperation.

I wonder, even in a fast and furious world, can we cultivate quiet souls? Can we be calm and peaceful and at rest on the inside, even when all around us are chaos and noise?

That thought is so appealing to me. I am all for hard work and being responsible, but I don't want to get to the end of my life and be known as a busy person. I don't want that to be the word that comes to mind when my kids and spouse and friends try to describe me after I'm gone. "He was busy. He was a hard worker. He always seemed kind of stressed out, poor guy, but he got a lot done."

There is value in being productive, of course, but I would rather be known as someone who loved life, loved people, and loved God. Someone who knew how to enjoy each moment and simply be at peace and rest on the inside.

One of the greatest examples in the Bible of a quiet soul is David, the most famous king of Israel. He was a warrior, politician, family man, visionary, musician, and songwriter. If anyone knew what it meant to face constant stress and pressure, it was David.

Yet David's most lasting legacy is not the empire he built, the enemies he defeated, or the laws he passed. Arguably his greatest legacy and gift are his songs, recorded in the book of Psalms. They are a heartfelt, passionate, authentic expression of his journey with God. And thirty-five hundred years later, his words and emotions still resonate with our souls.

I think this ancient king understood something that our frenetic twenty-first-century culture desperately needs. He knew how to have a quiet soul.

Psalm 131 in particular gives us insight into David's unique ability to maintain a quiet and restful soul. This psalm is part of a collection of fifteen psalms called the Songs of Ascent. They were traditionally sung by Jewish caravans on their way to Jerusalem to celebrate their annual religious feast. The Songs of Ascent were their road trip playlist.

Here are verses 1–3:

> O LORD, my heart is not lifted up;
> > my eyes are not raised too high;
> I do not occupy myself with things
> > too great and too marvelous for me.
> But I have calmed and quieted my soul,
> > like a weaned child with its mother;
> > like a weaned child is my soul within me.

*O Israel, hope in the L*ORD
from this time forth and forevermore.

Notice especially verse 2. David is intentional about having a calm, quiet soul. He values it, he seeks it, and he finds it.

Remember, David was a hero in Israel. He was a celebrity. He was the most influential and affluent person around. He had more power, fame, fortune, and responsibility than most of us could imagine.

Why is that relevant? Because David was a man before his time. He was in this ancient setting, yet he could relate to someone living in our age. He had everything at his fingertips. He didn't have a cellular device, but he had people who would serve him, do anything for him, and get any information he wanted. He had a fast-paced, loud life.

Yet somehow, even with all his opulence and popularity and fortune and fame, he found a way to quiet his soul. If King David could develop a calm soul in the middle of the craziness and chaos of ruling a kingdom, maybe there is hope for you and me.

I doubt David's soul was always quiet, by the way. I think he had his moments, just like any one of us. Actually, that is exactly why he wrote about intentionally quieting his soul—he clearly faced the same temptations we do to let our thoughts and emotions get out of control. But in general, he seems to have discovered how to live from a quiet space, a peaceful place on the inside.

OUT OF CONTROL

There are only three verses in this beautiful, short, potent psalm. But they give us several keys that we can apply today. The first verse starts like this: "O LORD my heart is not lifted up; my eyes are not raised too high."

That is a radical statement for a king to make, especially in that culture. He was the most powerful person in his nation. He would have been treated like a god. But he is saying in this psalm, "I know there is a God and I am not him. People treat me like a god, but I am not going to buy into that."

You might say, "I've got ninety-nine problems, but a god complex ain't one. No one worships me. I'm not a celebrity. I certainly don't think that I'm God."

But to some extent we all struggle with viewing ourselves as God in our own lives. We say things like, "It's all up to me. If this is going to happen, I'm the one who has to do it."

That's God language. Yes, we have responsibilities—but ultimately we aren't in charge of our fate. We can't control everything. Only God can.

David told God, "I'm not letting my thoughts get blown out of proportion. Yes, I am the most powerful man around; I am the king; I am the man—but I am not God. Lord, only you are God."

The principle here is this: if you want to have a calm, quiet soul, you have to recognize that you are not in control. That realization is fundamental to being healthy and peaceful on the inside. *I am not in control. I am not in charge. Ultimately, I am not dictating my days. God, you have numbered my days. You*

have ordered my ways. I make my plans, but you direct my steps.
Lord, I trust that you have my best interests in mind.

That's the opposite of what we usually think. We tend to assume that if we lack rest and peace due to the uncertainties of life, then the answer is to be *more* in control of our fate. If we could just prepare for the future a little better, if we just had a little more money in the bank, if we just had a few more safety nets in place, then our souls would find rest. We equate external control with inner tranquility.

But it doesn't work that way. No matter how hard we study or work, no matter how early we wake up or how late we go to bed, ultimately time and chance happen to us all. We can't guarantee anything.

But God can.

And *only* God can.

When we remember that, a peace that passes understanding floods our souls. Quietness and rest are found not in control but in surrender. The prophet Isaiah said exactly that to Israel hundreds of years later: "Only in returning to me and resting in me ~~return~~ will you be saved. In quietness and confidence is your strength" ~~to find~~ (Isaiah 30:15 NLT).

In our modern society and culture, ambition has almost been deified. It is celebrated, glorified, expected. How many times have you heard things like this: "You can be anything you want to be. Just believe. Whatever you put your mind to, whatever you put your heart to, you can do it and you can be it."

I'm sorry to break it to you, but that's not actually biblical. You can be who *God* called you to be; who *God* designed you to be; who *God* wired you to be. That might not sound like "the

In who God calls me to be?

American way," but it's the truth, and there is peace there, there is rest there, and there is ease there. *How do I know?*

I believe in ambition. Don't get me wrong. There is a lot to be said for goals, for a work ethic, for a whatever-it-takes attitude. But reckless, self-focused ambition might be one of the main reasons many people feel such angst on the inside.

Ambition that isn't tethered to God's calling tends to take on a life of its own. Often it turns into competition and comparison. Our focus becomes getting that job, that salary, that house. We hang our identity and value on achieving something we can't control. And deep inside we know we can't guarantee success, which is why we can never truly be at rest.

Is God really God? Do we actually believe he is in control and that he loves us? If so, then we don't have to play God. We don't have to be in control. We can find rest for our souls in quietness and confidence.

Yield your ambitions and dreams and desires to God. That is a safe place and a sane place. Let him be God. It's his job, and he's really good at it.

I DON'T KNOW

In Psalm 131:1 David went on to say, "I do not occupy myself with things too great and too marvelous for me."

Essentially he is saying, "There's a lot I don't know. I don't have all the answers. I don't know all the facts. I don't understand everything. And I'm okay with that."

This is incredible, coming from King David. How often do you hear a king, president, or political leader say, "I don't know"? But evidently David was comfortable with this kind of language.

Do you have an "I don't know" category in your life? Let me put it another way. Do you have a God category in your life? Do ◄—— you have a category where you put things that you don't understand, that you don't know, that you don't trouble yourself with? ◄—— What do you do with things that are too great and too marvelous for you and your finite, limited paradigm and perspective?

I don't know about you, but my brain has not been activated long enough to figure this universe out. I'd better have a God category in my life, a category where I can put the things that I don't understand and can't comprehend. How arrogant would I be if I pretended and intended to have an answer for everything?

I'm not so sure I am ever supposed to know all the answers, actually. And the older I get, the more I know how much I don't know. The more I recognize how much there is left to learn. And the more comfortable I am with saying, "I just don't know."

King David, of all people, had access to information. He didn't have Google or Siri, but he had an army of intelligent, educated, informed people at his beck and call. No one would have faulted him if he would have tried to have an answer for every question. It was expected of him, actually. He was the king, so he was supposed to be the ultimate source of answers, solutions, and insight.

But David said, "I will not try to figure out everything in my life. Some things are beyond my comprehension, and I'm not going to act like I know it all." He set lines and limits to his data and his information. David was making a profound statement about how to have a calm and quiet soul. He was saying, "I can't know it all; and furthermore, I can't handle it all."

That realization has never been more needed than in this age of instant information. For example, I'm not so sure that we were designed to have these cellular devices with relentless, simultaneous updates on every local, national, and global crisis. You can be in the cereal aisle at Safeway, trying to run errands and get your kids to soccer practice, and be updated six or seven times on tragedies and atrocities around this hurting globe.

I'm not advocating being coldhearted or indifferent or igno-rant. I'm all for staying in touch with current events, and we should allow our hearts to feel the pain of those around us. But I don't know if our souls have the capacity to comprehend and process all of the world's tragedies. I know God does, but I don't think we do.

We are all stewards of our own souls, by the grace of God, and we can set limits on what we listen to. Just because we *can* know something doesn't mean we *should* know it or that we should fret and fixate and focus on it. It's a fine line, a subjective line, a very personal line. I can't tell you what you are supposed to know—I can only define that for myself.

Do you want a quiet soul? Do you want a peaceful spirit? Then draw lines. Draw limits. Create a margin and a buffer for your soul. Every day there will be issues, topics, and drama that cross our paths but are not necessary for us to understand. These things are on a need-to-know basis—and we don't need to know.

Let me be very practical here: gossip is something you can

immediately eliminate. You don't even need to pray about that one. People around you undoubtedly have a few hidden secrets and closet skeletons that you just don't need to know. And if some well-meaning soul tries to inform you about something that is none of your business, just say, "Thanks, but I don't need to know that. I love him. I believe in her. I don't need to occupy my mind, will, and emotions with issues that God hasn't asked me to fix."

Drawing lines and setting limits isn't irresponsibility. It isn't selfishness. It's *wisdom*. It's okay if we don't know all the news and all the details, if we don't know about every person who is hurting in the world, and if we don't know all the gossip, because God is really good at being God. He knows everything, he is in control, and his grace is enough.

David—a king, a ruler, a man who needed to know more than most of us—recognized that, and he said, "I'm setting lines and I'm setting limits. I will not occupy myself with things that are beyond me."

A LEVEL SOUL

David continued: "I have calmed and quieted my soul" (Psalm 131:2). The Hebrew word translated *calmed* in this verse literally means "to make level."[1] It is used in the Bible in the context of leveling an uneven field (Isaiah 28:25). David was saying that he has intentionally leveled and settled his soul.

I think David was recognizing here that his internal levels were off sometimes, and it made him inconsistent in his soul. It happens to all of us, and David was no exception. He was aware of the perceptions of people around him. He heard the barrage of both praise and criticism. He was under never-ending pressure and responsibility and stress.

I think David faced the same question we do today: Do I live according to who I really am, or do I live according to who people perceive me to be or want me to be? *who I think I should be*

David was obviously popular. He was famous. He was a celebrity. The paparazzi were constantly trying to make sculptures of him. So David was saying, "I know people see me a certain way, but I have made a decision to level my soul and to live from who I genuinely, truly am."

You can see this throughout David's life. For example, the book of 2 Samuel records an incident that occurred when David orchestrated the return of the ark of the covenant to Jerusalem. The ark was a sacred box that represented the presence of God, and it had been gone for many years. When the ark entered the city, David was so excited and passionate about God that he joined with the multitudes in celebrating in the streets. He took off his kingly robes and danced in front of everyone in a simple priest's garment. It wasn't indecent, but it was certainly undignified.

People—including his own wife—were like, "What are you doing? You are the king. Stop it. You're embarrassing us."

David didn't care. He basically replied, "Really? You think this is undignified? I don't care. I love God, and I'll worship and celebrate him like I did back when I was just a lowly shepherd. I'm still that guy. I'm not too proud or proper or popular to be myself. This is who I am." David knew how to level his soul.

or act because of comparison

Surrender + listen
\
+ surround A QUIET SOUL *But who is that?*
How do I know?

It is imperative that we understand we do not have to live up to who people say we are or perceive us to be. By the grace of God, Jesus enables us to live from who we really are.

A lot has been written and publicized about the social media phenomenon the world seems to be swept up in. I'm not here to vilify it—I love social media. But let's be honest. How much time do we spend trying to look authentic? How much effort do we put into looking effortless? How many photos do we take and filters do we try in an attempt to look candid? It's a little comical, actually.

Most of us aren't celebrities, but we deal with some of the same strange issues that celebrities do because social media inherently pushes us to portray a persona worth following. Before we know it, we are caught up in trying to post things that other people like and in trying to be who other people want us to be, or maybe who *we* think we want to be, but in the process who we really are gets a little bit misplaced.

David was dealing with all that, and he tells us, "I need to level myself out here. I don't want to forget who I am. I don't want to become inconsistent and imbalanced in my soul."

He continually reminded himself, *I might be the king, but I'm still just David. I used to be a shepherd who lived simply and loved God deeply, and I was happy. Now my job title and influence have changed, but I'm not going to lose perspective. I'm still me.*

I think the greatest leveler is worship. I talked about this in the first chapter. Worship reminds us of who God is and who we are. It was one of David's secrets. He had his share of problems and mistakes, but he was a worshipper. And as his soul worshipped, it stayed level, grounded, and authentic.

It's funny how easily your soul can get worked up. People start saying nice things about you, you get a promotion, you drop those extra eight pounds and you are looking fit and feeling amazing and emanating this awesome image—and yet you have cracks just like everybody else. And then out of the blue you hit some challenges or pain in your life, but now you don't know who to go to because you have a persona to protect and an image to maintain.

It's not sustainable and it's not healthy. You can't live on a level you are not on. Instead, just live from who you really are. It's incredibly liberating, actually.

A quiet soul is far more valuable than fame and fortune. A level soul, a balanced soul, a genuine soul—that is a gift from God.

A WEANED SOUL

David ended his song with a very strange metaphor. He said, "I have calmed and quieted my soul, like a weaned child with its mother; like a weaned child is my soul within me" (verse 2).

I was reading this a while back and I got to the end, and I was like, *David, bro, what does breast-feeding have to do with anything?* That is how my brain works.

"I have calmed and quieted my soul"—*that's awesome, David, great lyrics*—"like a weaned child." *Huh? Why are we talking weaning now, David? That's kind of weird.*

And then he ends, "O Israel, hope in the LORD" (verse 3).

Why would David be inspired to give us a word picture of

a weaned child with his mother? I think David was saying two things with this metaphor.

First, keep in mind that David used prophetic, redemptive language throughout his writings. In other words, his lyrics don't just describe current feelings, but they also look forward to a time when God was going to send his promised Messiah. God inspired David and the other writers of Scripture to write things that pointed toward the future, toward Jesus.

I think David had a glimpse of what Jesus would provide for humanity. Hundreds of years later, Jesus used similar imagery when he told a man named Nicodemus that to know and follow God, he had to be born again (John 3:3).

David was saying, "If you want a calm and quieted soul, you have to understand that you did not earn God's love. You were born into it, like a child with his mother." A calm and quiet spirit is the result of understanding that our relationship with God is not based on worth but on birth.

Second, David was communicating the attitude we should take toward God. That's why he didn't just say "like a child with his mother," but instead threw in the descriptive word *weaned*. It was intentional.

Chelsea and I have three kids, and we breast-fed them all. Well, she breast-fed them. But these days, husbands claim everything. *We* got pregnant, *we* gave birth, *we* breast-fed—it's a team effort.

The thing with breast-feeding is that when the baby is awake in his mother's arms, even if it's not time to eat, he only has one thing on his mind: food. I saw this with all our kids, especially the middle one. He always wanted to eat. Still does, actually.

We would be in a restaurant, and Chelsea would be holding the baby. And inevitably, his little radar would detect the direction of the nearest source of milk. I don't know if it's instinct or habit or muscle memory, but he would start pawing and grasping. Chelsea would have to hold him at arm's length because things were getting inappropriate in public.

When a child is breast-feeding and he is in the arms of his mother, he wants milk. Unless he is asleep, he is never at peace.

David said two times, "I'm like a weaned child." What does a weaned child in the arms of his mother want?

Nothing.

That baby is just happy to be in the arms of his mother.

Do you know what David was saying? He was telling us that he has a calm and quiet soul because he is content with who God is. I think David was writing this song and he was saying, "I have fame, I have riches, I have opulence, I have influence—I have it all. But everything pales in comparison to you, God. I am like a weaned child, a child who spends time with his mother not because he wants something but simply because he loves to be close to her. I just want *you*, God."

By the way, God loves to hear what you want and what you need. The Bible says he already knows what you need before you even ask. So ask. You don't need to play games with God. "I want these five things, but I'm going to pretend that I don't so that maybe I will get them." He already knows, so feel free to ask.

But hopefully we can experience the space David was in here. Hopefully we can say, "What you do for me is awesome, God, but I just want to be in your arms. I just want to be with you."

So why fight it. doubt it.

We read Hebrews 6:19 earlier. It says, "We have this as a sure and steadfast anchor of the soul."

I love those first three words: "we have this." The writer of Hebrews used it to set up an explanation of who Jesus is and what he accomplished on our behalf.

Listen to that language: *we have this.* We don't have to go get it. We don't have to earn it or deserve it. We already have what we need. And we know that God will continue to provide what we need in the future.

But more important, we have a God who wants—with every ounce and fiber in his being—to hold us in his arms. We don't need an agenda or a to-do list when we approach God. He likely doesn't have much of an agenda either. He just wants to relate. He just wants to be with us, like a mom and her child.

Maybe you are wondering, *What exactly does that mean, Judah? Can you give me three practical steps to being in the arms of God?*

No, I can't. And I don't know if you need that, because I think you were designed for this. You were wired for this. Of all beings in the universe, you are the human being; you are the primary being; you are the object of God's affection and desire. You were designed to be alone with God, to enjoy God, to feel God, and to experience God. I think it is intuitive in your makeup and your system.

I think you simply have to let your soul go there, by the grace of God, and say, *Okay, God, here I am. I'm going to enjoy you.* When you are stuck in traffic, while you are running errands, while you are shuttling kids everywhere, when you are in a minivan or a grocery store or a cubicle at work, let your soul be like a weaned child within you. Let it go into that space where God is. Think about him; ponder who he is; maybe say some things internally that you don't say verbally. Let yourself just enjoy the embrace of your Maker and your Creator.

You probably can't—or shouldn't—quit your job tomorrow. You can't abandon your responsibilities or escape from the daily noise and pace of life.

But in the middle of all your coming and going and doing, you can, like King David, let God level and calm your soul. Even in a world where the volume is deafening and the velocity is dizzying, you can discover sanity, rest, and ease. You can discover a relationship with God that revolves around not getting things *from* him, but simply being *with* him.

And in that space, you will find a calm and quiet soul.

Surrendered +
Surrounded

seven

AN EFFECTIVE LIFE

When you were a kid, did anyone ever ask you, "What do you want to be when you grow up?" Maybe an aunt or uncle at a family reunion pinched your cheeks, commented on your height or hair length or acne, and then started questioning your career goals. You were all of eleven years old, but you were expected to have a logical, feasible, fiscally responsible answer.

I remember being in first grade and trying to answer that question. My teacher, Mrs. Paulson, asked us to draw what we wanted to be when we grew up. As we drew, she walked around and, based on our personalities and abilities, gently directed us toward career goals that were . . . realistic.

I had a desk next to Kelly, who was the love of my life at the time. I used to call her my honeybun, which is just weird. I was a hopeless romantic. Still am.

Kelly was sitting next to me, and I will never forget Mrs. Paulson coming by as we were all attempting to draw pictures of what we wanted to be in that far-off future known as adulthood. Mrs. Paulson stopped by Kelly's desk and said, "Kelly, what are you going to draw?"

Kelly said, "I don't know."

So based on Kelly's propensity and genius and capacity, Mrs. Paulson started suggesting things she could draw. "Kelly, you are so smart and so brilliant. You could be a mathematician, or you could be a professor, or you could be an astronaut. You could even be the president, Kelly!"

Kelly's eyes got big, and she started drawing as fast as she could.

Then it was my turn. "Judah, what are you going to draw?"

"Gee, I don't know, Mrs. Paulson," I said in my innocent and very, very high-pitched voice. "What do you think I could be when I grow up?"

Long pause.

"Uh . . . um . . . well, I don't know, Judah. Lots of things I'm sure. Let's see . . . well, you could be a good citizen. Yeah, you could pay your taxes and work . . . uh, somewhere? Doing something, I'm sure. You could have a family. Well, you'll think of something." And she hastily moved on.

I think I ended up drawing a picture of me saving a neighborhood cat, because that was the highest calling I could expect or aspire to. I can't blame her for drawing a blank. School was obviously a challenge for me. And overly honest Mrs. Paulson was just trying to manage my expectations.

I never ended up saving a cat, but I did survive school, and today I am a full-fledged adult with an actual occupation and family and income. So I think it's fair to say I exceeded Mrs. Paulson's expectations. She's probably very proud.

The experience makes me wonder, though. Why do we focus so much on what kids want to *be* and *do* when they grow up? It's a misleading question. It insinuates something completely untrue about life.

It insinuates that life is a *destination*. That life is about arriving. And more specifically, that life is about arriving at a profession, a job title, and a career.

For example, you become a police officer. Okay, you arrived. Now what? You discover that becoming something, in and of itself, is not the end-all. It's the beginning. Now you have to do the work of a police officer. You have to pull people over. People like me, who go a little over the speed limit and get ticketed.

I'm like, "Really? I'm one of the good guys. There are people out there pillaging villages, and you are pulling me over?"

Chelsea tells me, "You have an attitude problem, Judah."

"No," I insist. "They are wasting their time on me. I'm a good citizen. Just like Mrs. Paulson said I would be."

She says, "You were illegally speeding."

I say, "Don't say it like that. I'm just passionate. I'm trying to get somewhere."

Anyway, moving on. For some people, the goal isn't to reach a career goal—it's to get married. That is their benchmark for success. As if marriage were an end, right? No, my friend, it's just the beginning. The beginning of the longest, most excruciating, most blessed journey you have ever been on. I go to weddings and see these young couples getting married.

And everyone is like, "They are so sweet." And I am thinking, *They have no idea.*

I'm kidding. Mostly, anyway. I am in favor of matrimony. I am pro-marriage. I am happily and blissfully and irreversibly married. But as all married couples can attest, getting married is not the end. It's the starting gate. It's the qualifying round. It's only the beginning, and the best parts—and probably the worst parts—still lie ahead.

That's life, though, isn't it? Life isn't about arriving. We don't stop learning when we get out of school. We don't stop working when we get our first big career break. We don't stop dreaming when we reach a milestone. We never stop imagining; we never stop growing; we never stop reaching, believing, creating.

Life is a journey.

I think we should change the question. Rather than asking, "What do you want to be when you grow up?" we should ask a far more important question: "What do you want your life to look like?" Or maybe, "What kind of soul do you want to have?"

These are better questions; they are deeper questions. They are far more meaningful than asking what someone wants to do professionally or how much money he or she wants to have in the bank, because careers and cash are not the stuff of life.

This kind of question sparks an honest evaluation of how effective our lives are. Not effective in the sense of racking up monumental accomplishments or public acclaim, but in the sense of something simpler but less measurable: that of living lives worth living.

An effective life can look back and say, "My soul is full. I became who God made me to be. I did what God put me on this earth to do. I enjoyed life, I loved life, I made a difference. I had a full and fulfilled existence."

EFFECTIVE SOUL, EFFECTIVE LIFE

Our souls have a God-given need for purpose and significance. I think that's what we are subconsciously grasping at when we fixate on careers, titles, and achievements. A truly effective life, though, begins with an effective soul. It flows from a soul that functions and finds its value not in external accomplishments but in its relationship with God.

As our souls find themselves in God, our lives will find their purpose, place, and value in him as well. The apostle Paul wrote about this kind of fulfilled, effective life in his first letter to the Corinthian church. His concluding comments:

> I will visit you after passing through Macedonia, for I intend to pass through Macedonia, and perhaps I will stay with you or even spend the winter, so that you may help me on my journey, wherever I go. For I do not want to see you now just in passing. I hope to spend some time with you, if the Lord permits. But I will stay in Ephesus until Pentecost, for a wide door for effective work has opened to me, and there are many adversaries. (1 Corinthians 16:5–9)

Notice the phrase, "effective work" (verse 9). I read that a while back, and I started to think: *If there is effective work, there must also be ineffective work. There must be average work.* I don't know about you, but I want to spend the relatively brief hours, days, months, and years that I have on *effective* work, not on useless, mediocre, or unfulfilling work. I want to have a fulfilled soul and an effective life.

Throughout the Bible there are glimpses of what a truly effective life looks like. For example, notice what Psalm 1:3 says about a person who trusts and follows God.

> *He is like a tree*
> > *planted by streams of water*
> *that yields its fruit in its season,*
> > *and its leaf does not wither.*
> *In all that he does, he prospers.*

I love the metaphor and imagery the songwriter used. He didn't tell us how much money we will make, or what kind of job we will have, or whether we'll ever reach our ideal weight, or if people will ask for our autographs, or if we'll have more toys than our neighbors when we die. None of that. He said that our souls and our lives will be stable, faithful, passionate, fruitful, healthy, and blessed.

Psalm 92, verses 12–14, gives us a similar picture:

> *The righteous flourish like the palm tree*
> *and grow like a cedar in Lebanon.*

They are planted in the house of the LORD;
they flourish in the courts of our God.
They still bear fruit in old age;
they are ever full of sap and green.

This passage refers to "righteous" people. How do we become the righteous ones who flourish and bear fruit? According to the teachings of Scripture, it's not by being perfect. It's not the result of hard work or self-discipline. Righteous people aren't those who by sheer effort have made themselves a bit better than the people around them.

Instead, righteous people are those who trust in Jesus as their source of acceptance and righteousness before God. That's what Jesus came to teach us. We are righteous because of Jesus, and as we follow him, our lives begin to reflect these qualities and characteristics mentioned in Psalm 92.

Verse 12 says, "The righteous flourish." I love that word *flourish.* I want a soul that flourishes. Why settle for money in the bank when you could flourish? Why hang your happiness on a six-figure salary or a corner office or a bestselling album when your soul could flourish? Not that those things are wrong, of course. But you'll enjoy them a lot more if you are thriving and healthy on the inside, not just on the outside.

This passage says we will bear fruit throughout our lives and that we will be green and full of sap. I'm definitely not a plant person—I don't even know what plant people are called . . . Plantivores? Herbicists? But even I know that this is a good thing. The writer was saying that no matter what your age, you will have passion and youthfulness; you will be influential and productive; and in your marriage you will be sexually active to the end. Okay, maybe I applied that a bit too far. Don't be offended. I've said worse.

I want my life and my soul to be fruitful. I don't know what my paycheck will be in the future. I don't know what my bottom line will look like, or for that matter, what my waistline or hairline will look like. I don't know if I'll have a position or prominence or power. But I want to have a full soul. I want to have an effective, faithful, fruitful life.

Jesus returned to heaven at the age of thirty-three, but his years were full and fruitful. My dad passed away when he was sixty years old. He was young, but he had led an effective life. I don't know how many years I have left on this planet, but I want them to be the best years of my life. I'd rather live an effective life to thirty-three or sixty than live an ineffective life to a hundred.

An effective life cannot be quantified by how long you live, how many digits are in your bank balance, or how many people follow you on social media. Those things do not measure or define a person's life. An effective life has to do with the position and condition of your soul.

Are we effective, are we full, are we fruitful, and are we faithful? This is the life we want, but how do we obtain it? How do we find this space and place for our souls? How do we live in such a way now that when we reach the end of our days, we will be able to look back and celebrate lives well lived?

The apostle Paul's closing comments to the Corinthians give us two major elements of an effective life. I don't think Paul was trying to tell us his secrets—he was just concluding his letter. He was opening up his heart and giving practical help to the church at Corinth. But these two simple—but easily overlooked—elements to an effective life shine through in his writings because they were so ingrained in his lifestyle.

Keep in mind that Paul, formerly known as Saul, was not always effective. Before he came to know Jesus, this was a man who lived a very ineffective life. He was part of the problem, not the solution. He was involved in the arrest and murder of countless Jesus followers. His life was ineffective from God's point of view.

But then he had an amazing encounter with Jesus, which you can read about in Acts 9. Saul's name was changed to Paul, and his life almost immediately became effective. That's an understatement, actually. God used Paul to write thirteen books of the New Testament. Paul started at least fourteen churches, and those eventually multiplied into thousands of churches. He dramatically affected the philosophy and even the theology of the Roman Empire. Paul lived an effective, fruitful, full life.

It was also a life full of persecution, by the way. Paul faced more than his share of pain, misunderstanding, and resistance. There were people who didn't like him and who wrote mean blogs about him. There were people who tried to take credit for his successes, to undermine his efforts, and to discredit his motives. There were people who outright tried to kill him. His life was not free of pain or problems, but nonetheless, it was full, fruitful, and immensely effective.

I cannot promise that your life will be filled with nothing but rose petals and chocolates and cookies and cream. An effective life is not always easy and it's not always perfect. Sometimes things don't work out. There will be challenges and difficulties along the way. But in the midst of it all, you can still be full, fruitful, and effective.

A SURRENDERED LIFE

The first element of an effective life is woven throughout the passage I quoted above. Here are the verses again, with a few specific phrases emphasized.

> I will visit you after passing through Macedonia, for *I intend* to pass through Macedonia, and *perhaps* I will stay with you or even spend the winter, so that you may help me on my journey, *wherever* I go. For I do not want to see you now just in passing. *I hope* to spend some time with you, *if the Lord permits*. But I will stay in Ephesus until Pentecost, for a wide door for effective work has opened to me, and there are many adversaries.

Did you pick up the emphasis? *I intend; perhaps; wherever; I hope; if the Lord permits.*

"Paul," I want to ask him, "do you have any idea at all what you are doing tomorrow? Do you know what a schedule is? Get a Palm Pilot, buddy."

Palm Pilots are so outdated, you might be thinking. Well, ironically, that is the size of the iPhone now. Unbelievable. How does Apple do it? Someone texted me when the iPhone Plus came out and said, "This phone is so awesome and so big." And I thought, *What has happened?* We used to be all about small, and now we are all about big. The phone is huge. It's like a newborn baby: it doesn't fit anywhere. You never know where to put it. But we all love it, and Apple wins again.

Apparently Paul was not in charge of his own schedule. Notice, there are two *I wills* here: "I will visit you" (verse 5) and "I will stay in Ephesus" (verse 8). But there are five *if God wills*. He didn't use that exact phrase, but when he said *intend, perhaps, wherever, I hope,* and *if the Lord permits,* he was referencing his dependence on God's will, not his own.

In other words, Paul lived a surrendered life. That was how he functioned on a daily basis. It was the rhythm of his life. He said, "I am going to visit you—I think, I hope, I totally want to, if the Lord permits, if that's the Master's plan, if that's on his schedule—and I'm going to stay in Ephesus for now. God bless." An effective life is first and foremost a surrendered life.

Paul yielded his schedule, his decisions, his destinations, and his directions to God. Why? Because for Paul, God was not a formality or a tradition or a Sunday morning meeting. As I said earlier, once upon a time Paul was Saul, and Saul was a bad man. He was the mafia. He was a murderer. Saul was completely ineffective when it came to true living. He was on his way to hurt more people, and God basically knocked him off his donkey, shined a light in his eyeballs, and said in an audible voice, "Saul, what do you think you are doing?"

And Saul was like, "Who are you again?"

"I'm Jesus. The guy you thought was your opposition and competition. I have a team, Saul, and I want you to play on that team. As a matter of fact, I'd love for you to be the quarterback. Are you in?"

Paul was in. What would you do if you were blinded by heaven and heard God's voice? It was one of those no-brainer moments.

So for Paul, Jesus was real. God had physically confronted him and audibly spoken to him, and from then on, Paul's life was surrendered to whatever God asked from him. Paul's attitude was, "Wherever you want me to go, God; whoever you want me to talk to; whatever risk you want me to take; whatever prison they put me in; and whatever persecution I come under, I will do whatever you want me to do. I'm yours."

Some people think surrender is a sacrifice. I see surrender as the safest place to live. If God is leading, then all the pressure is on him. A surrendered life can say, "God, this is your fault. You're the one who got me into this mess, so you're the one who will need to get me out. I don't know what I'm doing here. I'm in way over my head. But God, I am totally surrendered to you. This is on your schedule, so this one is on you."

What a safe place to live, and what a beautiful place to live. We are just along for the ride. It's fun—and at times frightening—but ultimately the weight and pressure are on God, because we are simply doing his will.

A SURROUNDED LIFE

A surrendered life is a beautiful life, but unless you are intentional about staying grounded, it can backfire. Your surrendered

[handwritten margin note:] I don't know how to make that jibe with daily [illegible] responsibilities

life can become a really weird life. No offense, but I have met some people who are committed to living a surrendered life, and they are like, "I quit my job today, and I'm just walking the streets, and I'm singing."

And I want to say, "You can't sing, first of all. That's not your gift and it's not going to pay your bills. Let's go back to your boss and beg him to give your job back. Your surrender is scaring us all."

As we look at Paul's life, we see a second element of an effective life that is just as important as the first. Verse 9, which we looked at above, talks about "a wide door for effective work." Immediately after saying that, Paul wrote twelve concluding verses that focus on person after person in his life. He praises people, he greets people, he encourages people, and he connects people.

Verse 10: "When Timothy comes, put him at ease. He's so great. I love this guy."

Verse 12: "I really want Apollos to visit you soon."

Verse 17: "You've heard about Stephanas and Fortunatas and Achaicus. They are amazing. They are incredible. They have helped me so much."

Verse 19: "The entire church of Asia Minor, collectively, says hello. And Aquila and Prisca, who have a church in their house, send their love as well."

What was Paul saying? He listed seven specific friends he wants the church of Corinth to know, to care for, to meet, to appreciate, and to befriend.

Paul isn't just *surrendered*—he's *surrounded*.

Do you want to live an effective life? It's not as complicated as some might say it is. First, yield to God, your Creator and your Father. Turn over control of your ways and your days to him. And second, receive from the community that God puts around you. It's that simple. Stay surrendered and stay surrounded.

The Bible says, "God places the lonely in families" (Psalm 68:6 NLT). Don't underestimate how blessed we are to have people around us or how significant that community is.

Since I was a child, I have benefited from the church and the community of Jesus followers that surrounds my life. Somewhere along the line, by the grace of God, I surrendered to what God wanted for my life. Then God surrounded me with men and women, many of them have known me since I was a child, and those people have guided me, encouraged me, and helped me along the way.

You've probably heard that haunting proverb, "Whoever isolates himself seeks his own desire; he breaks out against all sound judgment" (Proverbs 18:1). In other words, if we are not surrounded, we'll tend to make dumb decisions. We'll be deceived by our passions and desires, and we'll end up hurting ourselves.

We weren't designed to be alone. We are relational beings. No matter how introspective or shy or private we might be, we are all designed for community. We are meant to benefit from one another.

How do you live an effective life? Yes, you surrender—but you don't do it alone. You surround yourself with other surrendered people, and before you know it, your life and your soul are fruitful and full and meaningful. Their words of encouragement, their text messages and e-mails, their silent support in difficult times, their counsel—they will change your life and build your soul.

I'm not the sharpest crayon in the box. I'm not the most avid reader or the best scholar. I'm certainly not the most self-controlled or self-motivated. But I can yield my life to God, and I can stay immersed in a community of people.

What a benefit and a privilege we have. We are here for each other: to surround each other, love each other, and encourage each other along this surrendered, yielded life. Surrendered and surrounded, we stay grounded. That rhymed unintentionally.

God is inviting each of us to have an effective soul and an effective life. His invitation is available to everybody. It's not going to be a life without challenges and difficulties, but in the end, we will be fruitful, faithful, and full.

eight

NEW YOU

This might be an odd question, but when you were growing up, did your dad wear a robe around the house? Mine did. I don't wear robes and I never plan to, so maybe it was a generational thing. But when we were growing up, after dinner and as the evening waned, Dad would inevitably wind up in a robe.

One particular night, I had an encounter with my dad and his robe. I was eighteen and I had been at our church's youth night. Afterward a group of us went to Red Robin. When you are eighteen and you go to Red Robin, you get a bacon cheeseburger and French fries and then you wash it down with a Mudd Pie, and your weight and waistline don't change a bit. Those were the days. I haven't had that meal since.

Anyway, we stayed out late. My dad knew I was at church, and he expected me to hang out with friends afterward, so things up until this point were fine.

Then one of the girls in our youth ministry who I thought

was kind of cool said to everyone, "Guys, I don't have a ride. Anyone want to drive me home?"

So I volunteered, "Yeah, I'll take you home."

This wasn't Chelsea, by the way. We weren't dating or anything, but as I said, I thought this girl was cool and I might have been interested in her. I took her to her parents' house. We pulled up and she was about to get out, but we started talking.

Now, we never did anything more than talk. I wouldn't have even held her hand, because my mom would have killed me, and then my grandma would have dug me back up and killed me again. Physical *anything* wasn't really an option for me.

We sat outside her house talking, and before I knew it, it had been two hours. We finally said goodbye, and by the time I got home, it was probably two in the morning.

I walked in, and I was dropping the keys off in the little bowl where my dad kept his keys, when all of a sudden I heard this loud, bass voice emanating from the darkness, "Good evening, son."

I think I squealed a little. I definitely jumped. I looked into the blackness and saw my dad, sitting on the couch in—you guessed it—his robe.

I don't know if your dad was like this, but for me, my dad was always bigger than life. He was an inch taller than me, his hands were larger, he had played quarterback in high school—he was my hero. And anytime there was a situation when he was being, well, *Dad*, my voice would go up an octave.

So in his low, ominously paternal tone, he said, "Good evening, son."

And I squeaked back, "Oh, hey, Dad! You scared me!"

I'll never forget it. I was just a big kid. It was two in the morning, the lights were out, there were eerie shadows all over the place—it was like a movie.

He said, "Son, why don't you come over here and sit next to me."

It wasn't a request. It was a command, which is indicative of my childhood.

So I sat down next to Dad in his robe. And he casually asked, "How was your evening?"

My voice still sounded like puberty had forgotten me. "Uh, it was good, Dad. You know, we were just hanging out at Red Robin and stuff. And this girl wanted a ride home, so I gave her a ride home, you know?"

"Who was it?" he asked.

So I said her name. He was like, "Well, that was nice of you. So you guys talked for a little bit?"

He didn't have to ask if we kissed or did anything else, because we both knew that wasn't an option.

Then he said, "Son, you and I both know she isn't the girl for you."

I was like, "Uh, well, I don't know, Dad. She's kind of cool. We had a good talk."

He was right, of course. He was always right. It was one of those moments where your dad is talking, and you know he doesn't want any kind of interaction. He just wants to tell you what's going to happen for the rest of your life.

He looked at me for a moment, and I looked back. He said, "You know, son, you're not the type of man who stays out late talking to girls you have no business talking to. That's not the way I raised you. That's not who you are. Son, be who you really are. Good night."

He stood up and walked toward his bedroom. The robe faded into the darkness. And I was left on the couch with nothing much to show for my life.

That was a defining moment for me. I was on the verge of manhood and independence, and I realized I had someone in my life who had enough authority and concern and love to tell me what I needed to hear. To tell me, "Hey, this is not who you are. This is not the way you were raised. You won't be happy if you go down this road. Stop doing what you're doing. Hey, son! Be who you really are. Good night."

Maybe you didn't have that luxury. Maybe you didn't have a dad or a father figure who would stop you in those defining moments and remind you to be who you really are. But for all of us, God wants to be that Father, that voice of authority, who reminds us who we are on the inside.

Why does this matter? Because what we think about ourselves is one of the most powerful forces in our lives. Do we see ourselves as failures? As quitters? As mediocre? Do we see ourselves as successful? As creative? As intelligent?

Our actions, decisions, and emotions are the natural result of what we think about ourselves. They flow from the perspectives we have of our identities. But often we don't stop to evaluate our self-perceptions. We don't think about who told us who we are or whether they were right or wrong in their assessments.

God wants to give *identity to our souls*. He wants to change us from the inside out and make us new people. He wants to help us see ourselves for who we are in him and then live accordingly.

Think about your identity and where you got it from. Much of who you are is a result of the family, country, culture, and environment you were born in. Obviously your choices play a huge part in shaping who you become as well, but there is something incredibly significant about birth.

Jesus told Nicodemus, a religious teacher who came to him for spiritual guidance one night, that if he wanted to know God, he had to be "born again."

That confused Nicodemus, who was probably expecting something more theological and less anatomical.

"How can a man be born when he is old?" he asked. "Can he enter a second time into his mother's womb and be born?" (John 3:4).

Nicodemus was missing the point. Jesus was saying that he needed to have a spiritual rebirth. He needed to have his identity reset on a soul level by God himself.

At its heart, Jesus' invitation to be born again is a call to receive a new identity. It's an invitation to join a new family. It is a spiritual but very real transition from living a life focused on self to living a life focused on God.

We are born again when we put our faith in Jesus and his work on the cross. In that moment, we become new people on the inside. Our souls are reborn.

I don't mean to sound spooky or hyper-spiritual. I don't really know how to describe it. But if you've experienced it, you know it's real. God brings new life to the inside you. You know he is real, you know he is there, and you know he loves you. And suddenly that invisible reality matters more than you ever would have understood before.

The soul's new identity through Jesus is one of the themes of the New Testament book known as Ephesians. Ephesians is a letter written by the apostle Paul to the Jesus followers in the ancient city of Ephesus.

In this letter, Paul, inspired by God, essentially sat down on a couch in his robe and said, "Let me remind you who you are. Let me encourage you to remember your identity, embrace your identity, and live according to your identity."

Let's look at four emphases in the book of Ephesians that dramatically shape the identities of our souls.

OUR POSITION IN JESUS

The first of these is found in the introduction to the letter.

> Blessed be the God and Father of our Lord Jesus Christ, who has blessed us in Christ with every spiritual blessing in the heavenly places, even as he chose us in him before the foundation of the world, that we should be holy and blameless before him. (Ephesians 1:3–4)

This is only a small part of an enormous sentence, at least in the original Greek. Paul piled phrase upon phrase, using more theological terms and concepts in one sentence than most of us try to swallow in a year.

Apparently he was a bit excited.

Why? Because he knew something about these brand-new believers that was going to rock their sense of identity—in a good way—and redefine them forever.

He was writing to tell them that they are now *in Jesus*. He spent the next six chapters talking about the new life of the believer, but he wanted to establish right from the outset that the way they get this new life is not through hard work or good luck or self-effort. It is by being in Jesus. He went on to use phrases like *in him* or *in Christ* more than thirty times in this short letter—I counted them.

This is the first emphasis I want to highlight in Ephesians because it has such a profound effect on our identities. Our stance and positions as believers is defined by the phrase *in Jesus*.

To be in Jesus means that our lives are defined by Jesus. It means that when God sees us, he sees Jesus. It means that when he evaluates us, he evaluates us based on who Jesus is and what Jesus has done. In Jesus, we are new creatures. In him, our souls have new identities. In him, we have blessings and benefits beyond what we could ever deserve on our own.

Honestly, that is amazing. Does God really see us and accept us and treat us like Jesus? This is hard enough to believe when you are reading the Bible or sitting in church, but it's even harder to believe when you just messed up for the fourteenth time. When your addiction has come back and it's worse than ever.

When your selfish actions have hurt those you love the most, and you can't understand why anyone would love you.

In moments like these, we desperately need to know that our lives are defined not by our successes and failures, but by our position in Jesus.

I talked with a friend a while back who told me that the first time his dad ever told him that he loved him was right before his dad died. My friend was thirty years old. He told me he always kind of assumed his dad loved him, but he had never heard him say it. So one of the last times my friend saw his father alive, he said, "Dad, I love you."

And his dad said back, "I love you too."

As my friend recounted the moment, emotion welled up in him. I could see what it meant to him to know that his dad accepted and loved him. Thirty years of wondering, and in an instant he knew he was loved.

I find that many Jesus followers are still unsure. *Does God love me? Is he for me? Am I okay? I've had a bad week—has God kicked me out of the neighborhood? Are we still on speaking terms? Am I out?*

Paul emphasized throughout this letter that our position before God is not defined by our actions, but rather by that simple phrase: in Jesus. We are chosen and accepted and protected in him. Our good behavior didn't earn God's acceptance, and our bad behavior can't unearn it.

When God the Father looks at us, he sees the Son, because when we put our faith in Jesus, his position became our position. We are set and seated in Christ. We are pleasing to God. We are loved by God. We are his forever. We are blessed with every spiritual blessing in heavenly places.

OUR SUPERIOR SAVIOR

The second emphasis that affects our soul-identity is found in the second half of Paul's prayer.

> [God] raised him from the dead and seated him at his right hand in the heavenly places, far above all rule and authority and power and dominion, and above every name that is named, not only in this age but also in the one to come. (verses 20–21)

The people who made up this community of Jesus followers at Ephesus were primarily brand-new believers. They had little or no understanding of the history of Israel or the Jewish people. They didn't grow up hearing how God brought Israel out of Egypt and made them into a great nation, or how one day a Messiah would come to save them. They were what the Bible calls Gentiles, or non-Jews.

Prior to following Jesus, they would have most likely been involved in the mystical, magical, superstitious environment of the day. Like humans everywhere, they would have been accustomed to trying to make sense out of life with nothing but materialism, logic, and human ideas to guide them.

What is the logical outcome of that kind of lifestyle? Sooner or later, it usually ends up producing fear and defensiveness. An outlook predicated on human understanding cannot produce confidence or a sense of identity because by definition, that outlook is as fallible and limited as our humanity.

These Ephesians had turned from following their own conclusions and superstitions and were instead following Jesus. Paul wrote with potency and urgency and passion to let them know the way they functioned before was not the way they would function with Jesus. Things were fundamentally different. Paul wrote to tell them, "Jesus is bigger and better than all those other gods and beliefs. You have a superior savior. You are following someone who not only *can* save you, he *wants* to save you and he *will* save you."

Paul told them that God's power is immeasurably great, that he is working on our behalf, and that Jesus is seated in heavenly places above any and every power and authority.

We read verses like these and we think, *God is amazing and big and powerful.* We assume God wants us to be in awe of how wonderful he is.

But I don't think that's the only reason these verses are here. God wants us to understand how great he is because his greatness has far-reaching implications for us. When we see him for who he really is, when we start to grasp how far-reaching and overwhelming his strength is, we can't help but face life with greater confidence.

This great God is on our side. We are not subject to the same chance and fate of every other human being on the earth. We have been transferred from the kingdom of fear, luck, self-effort, and darkness into the kingdom of light. We follow a God who is far above all authority and power, far above every name that is named, not only in this age but also in the one to come. There will never be a greater name than Jesus.

This is the God we follow. And if we follow this God, we are secure. We are safe. This God is reliable and he is trustworthy. We can find rest, we can find peace, and we can find ease in him. We will live differently once we understand this. It will change the way we see ourselves and our futures. We will begin to expect good things, because the God who rules the universe is with us and for us.

Many people are in favor of optimism, but this goes beyond optimism. I'm talking about trusting a real, personal God. A God who is good even when bad things happen. A God who is trustworthy even when life feels uncertain and random. No circumstance and no obstacle changes the fact that we have a reliable God and a superior Savior.

SO GREAT A SALVATION

When I was a kid, my parents were brilliant at hiding the fact that we didn't have very much money. I had no idea. I thought we had plenty of money. I found out later that my grandma regularly helped us out.

My parents didn't lie about it, and they weren't embarrassed about it. They just chose to focus on what we did have. So whenever we asked for something outside of their budget—"Let's go to Disneyland!" or "Let's buy a new car!"—they would just say, "We aren't going to do that right now. We choose not to spend money on that."

When I got older, I realized it was because we were tight on cash. But yet we were so blessed. Christmas was full of gifts, and I always had some Air Jordans—I just didn't know they were from Grandma.

I remember one vacation when I was about eight years old. We were in Sacramento, California, at my grandma and grandpa's house. It was beautiful, and it had a pool, and everything was amazing. My sister, Wendy, and I must have been developing a bit of an attitude about what they had and what we didn't have, because my dad sat us down for a little "talk." If there was one thing my dad hated, it was entitlement. No entitlement was allowed in our family. We were going to be grateful.

So he sat us down, and for an hour and a half he told us how good we had it. By the way, the danger in having a dad who is a preacher is that you're going to get preached to whether you choose it or not. Most people decide if they want to go to church and listen to the pastor, but the pastor's kids don't get that luxury. And if they don't comply and respond to the altar call, they are in danger of bodily harm. That's just how it works as a pastor's kid.

Dad told us about his own childhood and about how little money his family had. He said, "Kids, one Christmas we didn't have any money for presents, so we got pieces of wood and we carved toys for each other."

I was like, "That sounds awesome."

I was a slow learner.

He said, "When your mom and I got married, we didn't have any money. We lived for an entire month on granola and water."

I raised my hand. "Dad, did you eat the granola *in* the water? Or did you eat the granola and then drink the water?"

He said, "That's not the point, son!"

Looking back, I am so grateful for my parents, and I'm grateful for the gift of gratitude. I know we've all heard this before, but we need to remember where we've come from. We need to realize how good we have it. We need to recognize the progress we've made. Maybe we aren't where we should be or where we want to be, but sometimes we just need to stop and say, "Thank God I am where I am."

It seems to me that Paul was doing exactly this in Ephesians 2. This is where we find the third emphasis that shapes our soul-identity: *our great salvation.*

> And you were dead in the trespasses and sins in which you once walked . . . we all once lived in the passions of our flesh, carrying out the desires of the body and the mind, and were by nature children of wrath, like the rest of mankind.
>
> But God, being rich in mercy, because of the great love with which he loved us, even when we were dead in our trespasses, made us alive together with Christ. (2:1, 3–5)

He started out sounding a bit negative. He used terms like *dead, trespasses and sins,* and *children of wrath.* He wasn't in a bad mood. He just wanted his readers to fully grasp how far they had come.

Sometimes we like to think that we were doing pretty good before God, and then we found God, and then we got even better. In reality, we were dead and lost and helpless, then God found *us*, and he completely changed us.

We are new people, born anew from the inside out. We are not remodeled or whitewashed versions of our old selves. Our souls are born again. They have been made brand-new. You are a new you and I am a new me.

Verse 4 couldn't be clearer. It starts, "But God . . ." In other words, God made all the difference. Our lives were split in two like history itself: before Jesus and after Jesus. We used to be dead; now we are alive. We used to follow the passions and desires of the flesh; now we follow Jesus. We used to be children of wrath; now we are seated next to Jesus, adopted into God's family for eternity.

But God. That is the foundation of the gospel. It is the greatest revelation we ever need of God's love and care and concern for us. God found us and he saved us. He took the initiative and he provided the solution.

Paul continued, "For by grace you have been saved through faith. And this is not your own doing; it is the gift of God, not a result of works, so that no one may boast" (verses 8–9). He reminded these brand-new believers that their souls had been saved and their salvation was not in jeopardy. Back when they served idols and blind luck and materialism, they had good reason to fear. Those things could not promise them salvation. But Jesus is different. Their salvation was sure because it was founded on Jesus' finished work on the cross. It was by grace through faith.

Our hard work and good deeds and cleverness never could have saved us. Our salvation started with God, continues with God, and will be completed through God. If it's not our doing that got us saved, then it's not our doing (or lack of doing) that can make us unsaved. Salvation levels all humanity. It is by grace and grace alone. It is a gift of God.

Again, we have to stop being our own worst enemies. Our sins—past, present, and future—are forgiven. We aren't Christians because we live like Christians; we are Christians because we have accepted the gift of salvation. We have come to know God on an experiential, authentic level.

Yes, following Jesus produces genuine changes in our lives. That's inevitable. But our outward behavior and internal emotions might not always measure up to who we are on the inside. We are all in a process and we are all on a journey. At times we won't live like new people or feel like new people. But that doesn't change the reality that we *are* new people. Our souls have been born again.

Why is our salvation so great? Because it is a gift. Because it is God's doing, not our doing.

We have so great a salvation because we have so great a God.

WE BELONG

The first chapter and a half of Ephesians describes in breathless detail the stance of the believer in Jesus, the superiority of our Savior, and the significance of our great salvation. Then the letter shifts gears and focuses on the fourth and final emphasis that shapes our soul identities: the community in which we are set.

As I said earlier, these new believers were Gentiles. They were non-Jews, so they were on the outside looking in. But the instant they put their faith in Jesus, they became part of the family. On a spiritual soul level they went from being outsiders to being insiders. They were now part of a family that included heroes of the faith such as Abraham, Moses, Ruth, and David.

The Message paraphrases Ephesians 2:16–18 like this:

Christ brought us together through his death on the cross. The Cross got us to embrace, and that was the end of the hostility. Christ came and preached peace to you outsiders and peace to us insiders. He treated us as equals, and so made us equals. Through him we both share the same Spirit and have equal access to the Father.

That's plain enough, isn't it? Once you put your faith in Jesus, you're no longer a wandering exile. This kingdom of faith is now your home country. You're no longer a stranger or an outsider. You *belong* here, with as much right to the name Christian as anyone.

How powerful is that? We are part of God's family. We have spiritual ancestors, spiritual parents, spiritual siblings. We aren't outsiders looking in. We aren't interlopers or intruders. We have as much right as anyone to be here.

We belong.

The longer I pastor and the more I talk with people, the

more convinced I am that belonging is a fundamental need of the human soul. Many people are willing to do anything or sacrifice anything just to feel like they belong somewhere.

God wants you to know that you don't have to *do* anything to belong. You belong just as you are. You are already part of his family because of your faith in Jesus. You aren't on probation. You aren't conditionally accepted. Your case won't come up for review. You have already been accepted, and your acceptance is unconditional and irrevocable. That will shape and define your soul more than almost anything else.

Too many times as Christians we imply that people have to first *behave* and *believe* the right way before they can *belong* to our communities. We don't do it on purpose, but our actions and reactions when we see their flaws leave little doubt that they are outsiders.

We subconsciously create levels of Christianity. We call it spiritual maturity, but in reality it's a way to categorize—and ultimately either include or exclude—people around us based on arbitrary standards of conduct or Bible knowledge.

"Oh, that's your girlfriend you are living with? Not your wife?" We try not to look appalled. "Oh—okay. Um, congratulations?" And we wonder if we should tell them now or later that what they are doing is wrong and abominable and shocking. But we don't usually need to say anything, because people can sense our thoughts in an instant. They can tell that they don't quite measure up or that they aren't like the cool kids.

Meanwhile we might be struggling with lust or anger or pride on the inside, but since we've figured out how to keep our outside actions more or less in check, we feel like we are doing better than the guy who is still sleeping around or the girl who is addicted to drugs.

That's not the spirit of Jesus. He came to break down walls and barriers, not build more of them. He came to level the playing field.

With Jesus, we *belong*. Before we have done anything right, before we have all our doctrine figured out, before we get our lives cleaned up—we are his and he is ours. We are new creatures in Jesus. Our souls are made new. We have new identities.

And as a result of that newness, we start to *believe* the right things. We learn a bit of doctrine. We get to know the Bible. It might take a while, but the Holy Spirit teaches us and leads us into knowledge of God.

Ultimately we end up *behaving* or acting according to our beliefs. Our lives demonstrate real, lasting change. Not because we are so self-disciplined, but because our relationships with Jesus organically and supernaturally produce the change.

The biblical progression is first grace, then faith, then works. That is the divine order. God gives us his grace, and we respond in faith, and eventually our faith and relationship with God produce a healthy, holy lifestyle.

If we make behavior the qualification for belonging, we contradict the way God himself works. That's a scary thought.

Paul wanted these new converts to know—and God wants *us* to know—that when we began to follow him, we instantly became part of his family. We have brothers and sisters and fathers and mothers in the faith. Hundreds of generations have gone before us. We are surrounded by an immeasurable, uncountable family of Jesus followers who love, support, and believe in us.

The church isn't a building. It isn't a religion or an organization. It isn't a place to find spiritually themed entertainment or free child care on a Sunday morning.

It is a *family*.

God is building a home for hurting humanity where everyone is welcome. He is creating a community where everyone is loved, where everyone loves, where we serve each other and weep with each other and laugh with each other and do life with each other.

Some of the greatest challenges our world faces today are racism and discrimination. But imagine what a community like this could do to break down the artificial, irrational barriers of prejudice that fear has built. Imagine the reconciliation and unity this spirit of belonging would bring to lonely, rejected, hurting people. Scriptures like these could heal America. They could heal the world.

Jesus tears down the walls that we use to keep each other at a distance. The church is a safe place where we can be ourselves, even in our faulty states. We can come together and find healing, love, reconciliation, and forgiveness.

In Jesus, we are no longer alone. Our souls have been made new, and we belong to this great family.

Through Jesus, our souls are made new. We are redefined and reborn. God has solved the problem of sin and given us all we need to have healthy soul identities:

- We have our identities set firmly in Jesus, the source and definition of who we really are.
- We have a Savior who is superior to all authority and power, and he declares that we are blessed and approved.
- We have a salvation that is great, that is complete, final, and free.
- We have a community of Jesus followers where we belong even if we don't believe or behave exactly right.

In light of all that God has given us, we can face the future with a new security and confidence. In Jesus, you are a new you and I am a new me, and our souls are destined to thrive.

nine

INSIDE JOB

I was terrible at chores when I was growing up.

It wasn't my parents' fault—they tried many times to train their only son to be responsible around the house. My dad loved to draw and design, and he would come up with the most amazing chore charts. Visually, they were so motivating and appealing. I tried to use those charts. I really did. Every time he made one, I would fully intend to follow it. But within a couple of weeks, inevitably the chart would fall into disuse and disrepair.

Six months or so would go by, and my mom would decide—again—that I needed to help out around the house and learn character and develop a work ethic. So Dad would design another awesome chart.

That cycle was repeated pretty much until I got married. Now Chelsea is the one who tries to encourage me to be a contributing member of the household—again with little success. As I said earlier, I don't really do a lot of things with my hands. My wife recently gave me a Valentine card that on the front said something like, "To my bug-killing, car-fixing, plumbing-repairing, house-building husband," and I opened it up and on the inside it said something that I can't repeat but implied that I couldn't do any of those things but she loved me anyway. Basically I'm good at talking and at being romantic and not much else.

When I was a kid, there was only one chore that stuck. It was taking out the garbage. That was my one contribution to my family.

In our neighborhood, Wednesday was garbage day. Wednesday morning, to be precise, long before sunup. Naturally, I would always forget to take out the garbage until about midnight on Tuesday night. Worse, sometimes I'd wake up in a cold sweat at four o'clock Wednesday morning and realize that the sun had not come up yet, but the trash man would be there any minute. And if I didn't take out the trash, I was going to be in very big trouble.

The reason I'd get in big trouble was because when Mom was mad, Dad was madder. Dad was mad because I'd made his wife mad. I'm sure he was thinking, *My life is hard already, and you're making it harder. Marriage is difficult without you assisting me, son.*

I'm sure it's a similar dynamic in most marriages. The husband gets mad at the kids or whoever the culprit is because they ticked off the woman he sleeps with, and that never works out well for the husband.

So inevitably, I would take out the garbage in pitch blackness. Now, I don't like darkness. Didn't back then, and don't now. Some people enjoy the darkness. They embrace the darkness. That's slightly disturbing.

I prefer sunshine and light. I like to see what's happening. And if there is something out there that's going to kill me, I'd like a chance to see it coming.

Am I afraid of the dark? I didn't say that. I just said I don't prefer the dark.

We had two different-colored garbage cans. Every week, I would pull them approximately fifty feet from the house out to the curb. It was usually dark, as I mentioned, and because it was the Northwest, it was often windy and cold.

On the way out, though, I was brave. I was carefree. I had my eyes open and my head up, and I owned that driveway. Darkness? No big deal. I would arrange the cans, and then I would stand on the curb for a second and calmly survey the darkness.

And start to wonder what was out there.

And if it was dangerous.

And if it was getting closer.

Every single time, I would get spooked. I would tell myself, *There's no one there, Judah. No one is in the bushes. It's fifty feet to the house. Relax. You have the porch lights on. What is wrong with you, bro?*

And every single time, without fail, I would run as fast as I could back to the garage. I was on the basketball team during those years, but my fastest sprint times were always the late-night fifty-foot sprints to the safety of the house.

I would get into the garage as fast as I possibly could and press the button. Then I would huddle against the door that led from the garage into the house, waiting for the garage door to go down, and it never was fast enough. It was the longest wait of my week. It was like one of those dreams where you are in terrible danger and everything moves in slow motion except the bad guys. *Go down faster. Faster! He's coming! He's going to slip in! Aaaaggggh!*

Then I'd regain my emotional composure and walk into the house as if nothing had happened. If my parents were up, my mom would say, "Did you take out the garbage, Judah?"

"Yeah, Mom, no big deal."

Little did she know, my life was hanging in the balance for those fifty feet. What I wanted to say was, "Actually, Mom, I almost died again." Every Tuesday night I almost died.

As I think back on those weekly brushes with death, one thing stands out: how inconsistent my pace was. First I walked coolly to the curb; then I raced frantically for the garage; then I strolled nonchalantly into the house. No matter how hard I tried, I couldn't maintain a constant, consistent pace.

I've noticed that sometimes my journey with Jesus looks like my pace when taking out the garbage. There are days when I walk with such confident ease. But without notice, something changes in the circumstances, or my mind creates a scenario, and I go from walking to fleeing for my life. Some days I'm walking strong. But the next day—or the next moment—I abandon my steady pace and run away in panic.

The inconsistency in my soul, my walk, my behavior, and my relationship with Jesus is alarming at times. I start out as this confident, faith-filled person, but then I get one negative report and all of a sudden there is no God. We lose the Super Bowl on the 1-yard line, and suddenly I'm an atheist. It's amazing how inconsistent I am. Why can't I keep a steady pace?

A WALKING SOUL

Our souls need consistency. They need a steady walk and a regular pace. But the human soul is by nature inconstant. It is fickle.

The story of me walking the garbage can out to the curb only to run screaming back is just the human soul on display. One of the biggest issues our souls have to deal with in life is not the presence of negative circumstances, but the way those circumstances mess with our walk.

The Bible often describes our approach toward life and God using the metaphor of walking.

Walk in love, as Christ loved us and gave himself up for us . . .
Look carefully then how you walk, not as unwise but as wise,
making the best use of the time, because the days are evil.
(Ephesians 5:2, 15)

Paul told Ephesian believers that walking is the goal. Not running, not sprinting, not hiding, not fleeing, not escaping—just walking. That might sound a little boring, but in the long run it's highly effective. Just ask the tortoise.

Walking implies that our souls are experiencing steady, controlled progress. It means that we are moving forward. It means that rather than running for cover every time a threat appears, we are stable, we make good choices, and we have a positive outlook on the future. Steadily and surely, we are advancing.

Paul invited these ancient Ephesians to live a consistent life. Listen to his language. He said, "Look carefully then how you walk." He wanted his audience to take inventory for a second. He wanted them to ask themselves, *What does my everyday behavior look like? How consistent is it? What is my pace? Do I have enormous and horrible lows? Do I have days when my behaviors, thoughts, and feelings are dramatically different from other days? How influenced am I by my financial status? How affected am I by people's perceptions or gossip about me? How swayed am I by surroundings or circumstances or positive reports or negative reports or newscasts or phone calls from distant relatives? How consistent am I in my journey with Jesus?*

This is not a fun thing to investigate, frankly. It can very quickly become discouraging to look back on the week and ask yourself how consistent you were. If your disposition and personality are anything like mine, that is the last thing you want to do.

But that is just what Paul was saying we should do. "I want you to consider your lifestyle. Not your Sunday morning behavior—your everyday behavior. Examine the constancy and continuity of your soul's walk. Are you stable? Are you consistent? Are you doing what God wants? Are you making progress?"

Often, we'd rather talk about how brave we are. How much faith we have. How much love and hope and mercy and grace we have. Those are sexier terms than *stability* or *consistency*. And yet this passage is saying that we need to take careful inventory of our day-to-day walk.

I'M SURE

The word *walk*, as I said above, implies progress. The problem with progress is that it is often immeasurable and invisible. We don't like to think that, though. We tend to equate progress with reaching tangible, visible milestones. We want to measure it, quantify it, and predict it.

When it comes to our souls' walk with God, we want to see that quantifiable progress. We expect to be *better*: better husbands, better wives, better parents, better employees, better humans.

That will happen, of course. And when it does, it's awesome. As we spend time with God, we will advance. We will change and improve. But we have to remember that the point of our walk with God is not arriving. The point is walking. The point is being in relationship with God and experiencing life together. Growth and change are great, but they are not the main goals.

In our souls' walk with God, consistency is more important than growth. If we just stay the course, we will get to where God wants us to go. There might be a few switchbacks and setbacks and roadblocks along the way, but they won't stop us. God sees the whole journey from start to finish, and he's more focused on the pace and steadiness of our walk with him than on reaching some external milestone.

In another one of Paul's letters, this one to the church at Philippi, he wrote, "I am sure of this, that he who began a good work in you will bring it to completion at the day of Jesus Christ" (Philippians 1:6).

I read this a while back, and that first phrase stopped me: "I am sure of this." Paul seemed to have no doubts. He was totally convinced and confident that God would finish what he started in these Jesus followers.

My first thought when I read this was, *Am I sure of this for my own life?*

That's an important question to answer. Do we really believe that God started something on the inside of us and that he will complete it? If we are not sure, just imagine how unstable our lives will be.

I suspect that Paul wrote this because there were people in Philippi who were *not* sure of this. God wanted Paul to tell them that they could live with confidence and certainty because God was at work in them, and whatever God had started he would complete.

Sometimes I'm not too sure about the health of my insides. Is God working on me? Am I progressing? Is my soul healthy? What am I feeling and why am I feeling this way?

Then I wonder, if I can't even understand my insides, how can I determine if I'm actually making progress to a stable, more peaceful state? To be honest, I don't think the goal of our walk with God is that we would understand every quirk and reaction of our souls. The goal is that we would worship and trust and be sure of the One who *does* understand it all. He designed our souls, he is at work in our souls, and he will carry us through to completion.

God is working on the inside of you. Remember, when we

look at ourselves, we tend to think outside in—but God thinks inside out. God looks first at the inside. He is more concerned with our souls than our bodies.

He is in favor of our bodies, too, of course. I don't think he minds if we pray to keep our hair past our forties or lose ten pounds before swimsuit season. But his priority is our insides, because our insides affect everything else.

Christianity is primarily an inside job. Following Jesus is first and foremost an internal operation. God is changing us from the inside out. He is the only source of a consistent walk and a consistent soul.

I have to admit, I don't always live like I believe that. I say I believe it and I think I believe it, but many times I obsess over doing and becoming and achieving as if change were all up to me.

Human nature doesn't like to admit that our progress and our growth are in God's hands. We want to fix ourselves. And if we can't fix ourselves on the inside, we often settle for that cheap imitation called outward behavior. The end result of this approach is forcing ourselves—and others—to look and act a certain way. That is called legalism or self-righteousness, by the way, and it's not considered a positive character quality in Scripture.

Here is Philippians 1:6 again: "And I am sure of this, that he who began a good work in you will bring it to completion at the day of Jesus Christ." Let's look closer at what this verse has to say about the progress and constancy of our souls.

HE WHO BEGAN

First, notice the phrase, "He who began a good work." In other words, our walk with God starts with God. This is paramount. This is foundational. Our God connection started with God.

Sometimes we say, "I led that person to Jesus." That's great. But it's not true. Jesus leads people to Jesus. God connects people to God. It begins with him.

Let me take it a step further. The fact that you are reading this book right now, whether you call yourself a Christian or Jesus follower or not, is proof to me that God already initiated something in your life. God is working in you.

God gets all the credit, all the glory, and all the worship because everything begins with God. If you look at the Genesis account of creation, you realize this whole universe is for God, it's about God, and it's through God. We exist to worship and walk with God.

Begin is such an important doctrinal term. Everything begins with God. "In the beginning, God . . . " (Genesis 1:1). Everything we do is predicated on the fact that we trust and follow a living God, a real God, who is big enough to begin a process in the human soul and faithful enough to finish it.

This is rather foreign to the human mind and experience. We are used to taking what we want, to making things happen, to being self-starters and self-improvers. Sometimes it's hard to believe that God started this before we were even aware of him. God chose us. God revealed himself to our hearts. God drew us to him. Our progress did not begin with us, and it does not depend on us. It all goes back to God.

A GOOD WORK IN YOU

Where does God start this work? He starts *in* you and *in* me.

God is more than able to transform people on the inside. That means we don't have to force anybody—including ourselves—to believe, look, act, or talk a certain way. That is God's responsibility. That is his job description, and he is really good at it.

This can be frustrating, because a lot of us have discovered that a small dose of threats and condemnation goes a long way. We can guilt ourselves and others into making pretty significant changes.

So why wait for God? Why not just force change any way we can?

Because his kind of change is the only authentic, lasting, soul-level change. We can change the outside, but God alone can change the inside.

Jesus' harshest criticisms were for the Pharisees. These guys were famous throughout Israel as the best God followers ever. Their actions and doctrines were impeccable, and they made sure everyone knew it. Yet Jesus called them whitewashed tombs, blind guides, fools, hypocrites, snakes, and unmarked graves (Luke 11:44).

I think Jesus used such strong words because he saw genuine danger. Merely fixing up the outside might make us look good and feel good for a while, but ultimately it backfires. The paint comes off, and the cracks and faults are still there.

God starts deep on the inside, and it takes time to manifest on the outside. We tend to be in a hurry to fix the outside because the outside is embarrassing. The outside gets us in trouble. God plans to fix the outside—but he is going to take his own time to get around to it.

WILL BRING IT TO COMPLETION

Whatever God starts, he finishes. Think about that. You can't find one place in the Bible where God started something and said, "Actually, I've changed my mind. I lost interest. This is too much work. I'm out."

Now, if you are like me, I've started many things that I haven't finished. I have no idea how many things I've started and then thought, *I'm bored.*

Not God. He finishes what he starts.

In one of the last verses of the Bible, Jesus says about himself: "I am the Alpha and the Omega, the first and the last, the beginning and the end" (Revelation 22:13). In other words, this is so inherent to who God is that he calls himself the start and the finish. He names himself the A to Z. God is the beginning and the end and everything in between.

If God started a work in you, you can be sure he intends to complete it. Your hang-ups and mess-ups don't take him by surprise. At no point in the process does he say, "This is more than I expected. You are in worse shape than I thought. I'd better cut my losses and give up on you."

God has you in a process, and he is probably less worried

about your progress than you are. He can see the end from the beginning. He sees the whole panorama. You might not feel like you are progressing, but you are.

Just keep walking. Allow your soul to be directed and guided by God. He is faithful, and he will work in you and on you for the rest of your life.

Someday, "the day of Jesus Christ," as Philippians 1:6 says, this life and this walk will be over. God promises to guard you and guide you through life until that day appears.

DO YOU LOVE ME?

This brings us to Peter, one of the twelve guys Jesus rolled with for three and a half years. Peter is a perfect picture of the journey of the human soul. In the Gospels, Peter seems to have had a leadership role among the other disciples. He was a fisherman, a blue-collar worker. He probably didn't come from wealth or privilege.

Jesus called Peter, and God started working on the inside. Almost illogically, Peter dropped his nets and gave up his entire business. This probably would have been a family business that his dad had passed down to him, so there was a legacy and a reputation there. Yet Peter, at the words of Jesus, dropped his nets and left everything to follow Jesus.

Peter was outspoken, to say the least. He had a tendency to talk when he probably should have kept quiet. There is much recorded in Scripture about Peter's awkward comments.

One of these is found in Matthew 26. This is the story of the Last Supper. Maybe you've seen the painting.

As Matthew tells the story, right after the Last Supper, they sing a song. I can't imagine that Peter had a good voice. It just doesn't go with his persona. I have no idea if that's true, but that's how I see this in my head.

So Peter is belting it out, and then Jesus quiets everyone and says, "I need to tell you guys something. It's about to go down. I am going to do what I came here to do. I am going to die. Then you are all going to abandon me."

Peter can't contain himself, and he sputters, "No! I won't abandon you! Even if these other eleven clowns here leave you, I will not! I'm your man, Jesus. I'll be with you to the end, even if I have to die for you."

"Peter, you are going to deny me tonight, actually. Three times."

Hours later, Jesus is arrested. Peter finds himself at a bonfire outside the county jail, and a servant girl says, "Hey, you were with Jesus, right?"

"No!" Peter says emphatically. "I've never met the guy."

Really? He just denied Jesus to a junior high girl. Junior high girls can be intimidating, but this is crazy. Peter disowns the man he swore to love and protect until death. Later he will go on to deny Jesus two more times, just as Jesus predicted.

Talk about fickle human souls. In one night Peter goes from "I will die for Jesus" to "I don't even know the man."

Has this ever happened to you? What comes out of you makes you question what's inside of you. You say something, or you make a decision, or you do what you vowed you would never do. You seem to have no willpower, no courage. Moments ago you told people you would never, ever do this—and now you are doing it.

Sometimes in these moments, we ask some deep, dark questions. Things we might not say out loud, but we ask them of ourselves. *Is this real, or is this just empty religion? Is this a scam? Am I really different? Have I changed? Is Jesus real, and is he doing anything at all in me? Because I feel like I haven't progressed at all since I first met him.*

As those words were coming out of Peter's mouth, imagine what was going through his mind. *What? Am I actually saying this? Maybe I'm not a follower of Jesus. I thought I was, but maybe I was wrong. How could I have done such a thing? What is wrong with me?*

I was a youth pastor for ten years, and many times I heard young people say things like this to me. "I'm no different than before. This isn't working. This isn't real, and I don't think it ever was. This isn't for me. I'm out."

We've probably all been there. That is certainly where Peter found himself after his colossal, public failure. So he did what the inconsistent human soul often does under pressure: he ran away.

Jesus was tried, condemned, crucified, and buried. And then, three days later, he came back to life. It is the greatest surprise ending in human history. Over the next few days, Jesus appeared several times to different people, including the disciples themselves.

Apparently, though, poor Peter was going through such

extraordinary emotions that he decided to go back to his old occupation. Maybe he decided he wasn't cut out to be a disciple. Maybe he was too embarrassed by his mistakes to face Jesus. Or maybe he just needed to clear his head.

So Peter and some of the guys fished all night. John 21 contains the story told by the apostle John. It is an eerie repeat of an earlier episode in their lives. They catch nothing all night, and then a stranger on the shore tells them to throw their nets on the other side. They end up catching a ridiculous number of fish, and suddenly John figures it out. "It's Jesus!" he yells.

Jesus always did have a flair for the dramatic.

Peter jumps in and swims to shore. Jesus fixes them fish for breakfast. No one is asking any questions—they just look at Jesus while he serves them.

Then Jesus says, "Simon." That was Peter's old name. The name he went by before he met Jesus.

What is Jesus doing? Is he making fun of Peter? Is he saying he was still the same person as before? No—I think it's the exact opposite.

I think Jesus was reminding Peter of when they first met. The name Simon means "reed." Jesus is saying, "Simon, I remember when you were an average, ordinary guy. I knew you when you were a reed in the wind. I knew your humanity and your weaknesses. I knew you'd mess up a few times. And I called you anyway."

"Simon, son of John, do you love me more than these?"

Peter responds, "Yes, Lord; you know that I love you."

Jesus says, "Feed my lambs."

They go through essentially the same dialogue two more times. Each time, Peter insists, "You know that I love you."

I don't think Jesus is questioning Peter's love at all. He knows Peter loves him. The real question is, does *Peter* know that he loves Jesus?

I think Jesus was trying to remind Peter that his walk with Jesus was real. Despite Peter's frailties and mistakes, despite the conflicting emotions, despite the contradictory words and actions, God was at work in Peter. He was no longer Simon the reed—he was Peter the rock. For a while he hadn't acted like a rock, but that was still how Jesus saw him. And Jesus had a future and a destiny and a calling for Peter.

I'm sure Peter had his doubts. But Jesus lovingly, patiently helped him back on his feet. He helped him see himself as God saw him.

Isn't it amazing how we can talk ourselves out of a heavenly reality? In moments when we don't feel like our souls are making progress, when we wonder why our walk is so inconsistent, we need the same confidence Paul had when he wrote to the Philippians: "I am sure of this—God will finish what he started."

Notice that when Jesus found Peter on the beach, he didn't ask him if he was brave. He didn't ask him if he was committed. He didn't ask him if he was self-controlled. He didn't even ask him if he was sorry.

He simply asked him if he loved him.

There is a message in there for you and me. Our souls might falter at times, but our relationships with God are real. God put this love in our hearts for him, and it will only grow. Even when our emotions and actions betray us, God knows our hearts. He sees the seeds he planted in us and the work he began in us. And he has a plan to bring us to completion.

Are you sure of that? No matter what you have done, what you are going through, or what you will do, are you certain that the God who started a work on the inside of your soul will finish what he started?

That certainty will give you sanity. It will give you consistency. It will give you health on the inside.

ten

HEAVEN

If you have children, do you remember when you didn't?

Neither do I. Sleep deprivation does that to your memory.

I do know that before two people get around to propagating the species, life is different. Things are simpler. Quieter. More hygienic. Before you have children, every night is date night. Life is one perpetual date. Dating and mating—that is marriage without kids. Is that awesome or what?

The irony is that until you have kids, you don't know how good you have it. You think you know, and you think you are ready. But nothing completely prepares you for having a third human invade your lives.

I'm joking. I love my kids. God has only given them to me for a season, which is one more proof of his grace. Someday they will grow up and move out, and we will miss them, but they will come visit and that will be enough. Our plan is to lead our church for another twenty-plus years, and then Chelsea and I will move to Palm Desert and just enjoy being with each other every day. It's the circle of life. Hakuna Matata.

For four and a half years, Chelsea and I were married without children. Then we had Zion, our firstborn. He was born six weeks early, just to make the transition that much more emphatic. So not only were we unprepared in the sense of "we've never had to be responsible for another human before," we were unprepared in the sense that we didn't even have the nursery ready or own a car seat.

Because he was a preemie, he spent two weeks in the hospital, mostly in an incubator. When they finally let us take him home, I strapped him into his car seat, which was a process in itself.

I vaguely recall that before kids, when we wanted to go somewhere, we just got into our car and drove off. And when we got to our destination, we simply got out of our car and walked in. Gloriously uncomplicated.

Once you have kids, though, you have to prepare yourself emotionally and mentally when it's time to leave the house, because now there are special contraptions designed to protect them while in moving vehicles. They are not simply car seats, though. Not anymore. They are miniature spaceships. We tie our offspring down with nineteen different straps, and we cinch them all tight. And they scream and kick as we say through gritted teeth, "This is good for you!"

On that initial drive home, though, I was grateful for the spaceship car seat. Because I was suddenly aware that the roads were overrun with madmen driving massive metal machines.

My sweet, fragile son was in mortal danger. I think I drove twenty-five miles per hour the entire way to our house. Chelsea asked, "What is wrong with you?"

I was like, "The world is so dangerous!"

A couple of weeks later, when he was four weeks old, we decided to go out for lunch with Chelsea's sister Stacey. We went to the Dirty Bird—aka Red Robin—for old time's sake, because during her pregnancy with Zion, Chelsea constantly craved Cajun Clucks (aka chicken fingers) with blue cheese and extra-crispy fries. We ate that every stinking day.

It was raining, so I pulled up right in front to let Chelsea and Stacey out at the door. Chelsea had just pumped out a human, after all, and I didn't want her to stress anymore. Then—amazing husband and father that I am—I parked the car and ran back through the rain to the restaurant.

I got to our table. I sat down. The two ladies looked at me with an expression I couldn't quite understand, like something was amiss. Was it because I was soaking wet? Were they admiring my manliness and leadership and chivalry?

At that point Stacey, who was a little further along in the parenting process than we were, asked the obvious: "Hey, Dad, where's your kid?"

I raced back out of the Dirty Bird. I might have knocked over Red Robin himself. As I was running through the rain to the car, I heard a siren. *That's it*, I remember thinking. *Someone reported an abandoned baby. Four weeks into parenting and I'm already going to jail.*

But apparently the police officer was heading somewhere

else, because I got to the car and no one was there. No one except my poor precious preemie asleep in his spaceship. Stacey still won't let me forget that day.

Here's my point: learning to take another person into account is an adjustment. There is a steep learning curve involved with opening your heart and life to someone else. In the same way, taking God into account is an adjustment. When your soul starts to consider an eternal God who is intimately involved in your day-to-day existence, things change. There is a learning curve, and there are shifts in your thinking and priorities.

Let me explain. Before Jesus, we all had one priority: ourselves. Life was about being happy, about surviving and thriving, about getting ahead. It was about doing what we wanted. That's human nature.

But Jesus changes things. It's inevitable. Whether you've been a Jesus follower for years or months or weeks, or whether you aren't sure you even believe some of what I've written about in this book, Jesus has a way of shifting priorities and focus. The more we consider Jesus, the more we realize life is not just about ourselves. Life points to God.

As I said in the first chapter of this book, our souls are home when they return to God. Yes, God cares about our happiness; but he knows we will only find true and lasting satisfaction when we make him the focus of our existence.

That takes some getting used to, to be honest. It takes some intentionality. We have to learn how to take God into account, because for much of our lives, he hasn't been part of the equation.

AS IT IS IN HEAVEN

This process of taking God into account, this process of letting him help and heal and fulfill our souls, has been the theme of this book. But adjusting to the reality of God is not just about the decades we spend on this planet. The decisions and changes and shifts that occur in our lives are far bigger than this life.

Our souls are eternal. That's what the Bible teaches. Our souls had a beginning, but they will have no end. We don't just cease to exist. This physical body and existence will end, but the inside you and the inside me are going to be around forever.

If you ponder that for a moment, it's enough to blow a cerebral circuit. We are used to things having a defined starting and ending point. When something bad happens, we say, "Don't worry, this will pass." When something good happens, we say, "All good things must come to an end."

But by definition, forever will never end. Most of the time I can barely think beyond next weekend, much less comprehend eternity. I'm lucky if I know what I'm doing for lunch—how can I make plans for forever? And yet thinking about eternity is one of the healthiest things I can do for my soul.

I'll prove it to you. You've probably heard of the Lord's Prayer. Maybe you've even memorized it. It is found in Matthew 6. Jesus was teaching his disciples to pray, and he gave them a model prayer, an example of how they could pray.

There is nothing magical about this prayer. It's not an incantation we repeat to get God to give us what we want. Rather, it's an illustration of how candid and practical and confident our prayers to God should be. Here are the first few lines:

> *"Our Father in heaven,*
> *hallowed be your name.*
> *Your kingdom come,*
> *your will be done,*
>   *on earth as it is in heaven." (verses 9–10)*

Jesus is saying that when we dialogue with God, we need to consider where our Father is: he is in heaven. Jesus is saying, "I want heaven to be on your mind when you talk to God." Why is that important? Because earth is what consumes our minds more often than not. Even when we approach God in prayer, we often do so from a limited, finite perspective. We see the size of our problems instead of the size of our God. We see our weakness instead of God's strength.

Jesus continued, "I want you to pray that God's kingdom would be established and his will would be done on earth *as it is in heaven.*" That phrase "as it is in heaven" has latched on to my life and won't let go. That thought should be the theme of Jesus followers around the world. We are to live in light of the reality of heaven. Our lives should be framed by the phrase "as it is in heaven."

Here is one more scripture. Paul wrote this to the Colossian church:

If then you have been raised with Christ, seek the things that are above, where Christ is, seated at the right hand of God. Set your minds on things that are above, not on things that are on earth. For you have died, and your life is hidden with Christ in God. (Colossians 3:1–3)

Paul and Jesus were communicating the same thing: we are to orient and organize our lives around heaven's reality.

I don't know about you, but I am really good at organizing my life around earth's reality. It's easy. Jobs, appointments, bills, aches, pains, frustrations, annoyances, relationships, vacations, retirement—it's natural to build our lives around these things. It's our default.

But these verses tell us that things have changed now. For those of us who have put our faith in Jesus, our souls have been made alive. Now everything is different. We don't have to live like we did before. Now our lives revolve not around earthly priorities and problems and passions, but around heaven. We can structure our lives taking eternity into account.

HEAVEN NOW

I'll be honest—I've left heaven in the car a lot. I've forgotten that my reality has expanded and my focus has shifted. There have been many times I've started to orient my life once again around what I see, touch, feel, and hear. Thank God for people—usually my wife—who say, "Judah, where is heaven in all of this? Where is Jesus?"

Keeping heaven on our minds is healthy for our souls. We

are coming full circle with this, because again, I started this book by stating that our souls find their homes in God. But the ultimate goal for our souls is not to spend a few decades with God on this pained, polluted planet called Earth. It's to spend eternity with him in a place called heaven. Our souls find their homes in God, and heaven is the context in which that relationship will flourish long after this life ceases. Therefore, our souls are healthiest when they are focused on the reality of an eternity with Jesus.

Our souls need heaven.

Most of us probably don't spend much time thinking about heaven. Why? Because earth gets in the way. Earth is present and all too tangible. Our five senses are constantly aware of its reality. But heaven is eternal, ethereal, invisible. Maybe that's part of the reason we forget heaven—we can't wrap our brains around it.

For many people, the word *heaven* conjures up images of chubby babies playing harps on clouds. That's weird, physically impossible, and totally unappealing. I don't want to play a harp in a diaper. Ever. And I hope to God my eternal body doesn't look like a Huggies commercial. I'm hoping more for Wolverine.

Other people visualize heaven as a never-ending church service. That's not very exciting either, if we are honest. I've attended more church services than I can count, and a few of them have definitely felt eternal. And not in a good way. I remember thinking, *If this is what heaven is going to look like, I'm not sure I want to leave earth. This feels more like the other place.*

Sorry—that's terrible. Even if it is true. But my point is that heaven is not going to be torture and it's not going to be boring.

How do I know that? Just look at earth. Overall, this life is awesome. Even in a world deformed by the presence of sickness, pain, evil, and death, life is still amazing. It has pleasure, joy, excitement, and fulfillment. I realize there are people whose lives are *not* characterized by those things, and I don't mean to demean their suffering. They might not agree that life is good. But I think most of us can at least see the potential that this earth has. We have moments and seasons of enjoyment that give us a taste of what life could be like if sin and pain would stop getting in the way.

If earth has so much to offer, heaven will not be a downgrade. Heaven will be what earth was never able to be because of sin, and more besides.

The book of Revelation is one of the most dramatic, descriptive books of the Bible. It was written by the apostle John while he was living in exile for his faith on Patmos, a prison island off the coast of Greece. John is recounting a vision he had, apparently after eating some wild mushrooms he found on the beach. Again, I kid. But it is a very vivid and colorful book, so it makes you wonder.

If you can make it through the descriptions of battles and beasts, you get to chapters 21 and 22, which are absolutely amazing. They paint a picture of our souls' ultimate destination: eternity in heaven with Jesus. John's descriptions are spectacular. When you read, you can tell he can't fully describe what he saw in his vision. He is at a loss for words and metaphors. Human senses, terminology, and experience are not enough for us to fully comprehend what God has prepared for us for eternity.

Heaven is beyond our finite understanding, but that doesn't mean it is unimportant or irrelevant. Actually the opposite is true. The existence of heaven gives us perspective on earth.

That is precisely why Jesus encourages us to think and live and pray about this earth from the perspective of "as it is in heaven." Like Jesus, our lives should be dramatically impacted by the reality of eternity and heaven, because that is our ultimate home. This earthly existence is but for a moment. Heaven is eternal. We are to live our lives preoccupied by eternity.

John 3:13 says this about Jesus: "No one has ascended into heaven except he who descended from heaven, the Son of Man." Jesus *came from* heaven and he *returned to* heaven. In other words, the thirty-three years or so he spent on earth were bracketed by eternity. He lived here knowing where he came from and where he was going. Heaven was on his mind all the time.

Jesus lived from heaven to earth. He thought about heaven first, then earth. He looked at what mattered above, and he let that define his values and emotions and decisions down here. His life and ministry and teachings on this tiny planet floating in the Milky Way were profoundly framed by his heavenly perspective.

If we are going to live like Jesus, we need to think about heaven more. It's as simple as that. Ironically, when it comes to our passions and priorities, we often live as if this planet were forever and heaven were temporary. Jesus came to show us a new way to be human, a new way for our souls to approach and process life.

I really believe forever matters today. I believe that the

thought of eternity, of the bliss we will experience, and of the eternal love and presence of God can help put our pain and problems in their proper proportion.

I know I lost my job, but I'm not going to lose my mind. I know that my relationships are a little unstable right now, but God is faithful. These things will pass. My future is sure and my eternity is guaranteed.

We find peace, stability, and sanity for our souls when we frame our existence in the context of heaven. Heaven is not some ambiguous, random concept that will only make sense on our deathbeds. Heaven can serve us today as we consider the brevity of this life and determine to live in light of eternity. Life's complexities and challenges would be far less complex and far less challenging if we could approach every day like Jesus did: from heaven to earth.

What would our average, daily comings and goings look like if we lived that way? I'm not just talking about how we pray. I'm talking about brushing our teeth and filling up our cars with gas and working our nine-to-five jobs and taking juice packets to our kids' soccer teams. I'm talking about doing what fills our ordinary, everyday lives, but doing it while continually contemplating eternity in heaven. I wonder how that would affect our talking, our walking, our living, our socializing, our marriages, and our kids.

The more we live from heaven to earth—that is, the more we orient and adjust our lives to take eternity into account—the healthier and happier our souls will be.

KEEPING IT CLEAR

I said earlier that as we make room in our lives for Jesus, we realize that life is bigger than us. We see that it's about more than our needs and pursuits. Life starts with God, ends with God, and points to God.

The description of heaven in Revelation 21 and 22 is a clear illustration of this. In these chapters, heaven is symbolized by the city of Jerusalem. You'll notice that, again and again, this city is described using phrases like "clear as crystal" or "like transparent glass." Even the streets, which are made of gold, are transparent.

Why? I think chapter 21, verse 23, gives the answer: "And the city has no need of sun or moon to shine on it, for the glory of God gives it light, and its lamp is the Lamb."

I think heaven is transparent so that God can be seen more clearly.

The ultimate theme of earth and heaven is God. He is the focus of this life and the life to come. His glory fills heaven. His justice pervades heaven. His love permeates heaven. The power of God is all that will be necessary to fill the universe forever with brilliant, radiant light. That is how magnificent, glorious, generous, and gracious God is. He saturates eternity. All of heaven is shaped by him.

If God's presence and glory and goodness illuminate heaven, they should be the focal point of earth as well. So if you are a first grade teacher, let the glory of God shape your teaching. Teach those first graders like nobody has ever taught first graders before. And through that, God will receive glory.

If you are a barista—and there are a lot of them here in Seattle—greet your customers as if each one is the unique love and possession of God himself, because that is the truth. Learn their names and care for them and make drinks like no barista has ever made drinks before, because your barista-ness reflects God's glory, and by making a triple tall latte, you are adding to God's glory.

If you are a landscaper, mow lawns like no one has ever mowed lawns before. Make edges so sharp that your customers are flabbergasted because your lawn mowing is shaped by the glory of God. You will add to his glory with your passion and creativity.

If you are a painter, paint with all your heart. Paint in ways no one has explored, with colors and textures and boldness and innovation, and may your art be molded and formed by his glory.

If you are a stay-at-home parent, love your kids and pay your bills and administrate your household, knowing that what you do when no one is watching or applauding is going to make a difference for generations to come. You are a hero, and you reflect God's glory in everything you do.

If you preach, preach. If you write books, write books. If you fix cars, fix cars. May everything you do be shaped by the brilliance and majesty and magnificence of God.

When your life is shaped by God's glory, there is a good chance that some people will say you are crazy. They might say you've gone too far. But you have tasted and seen that the Lord is good. You have experienced just a portion of his greatness, his essence, his beauty, and his majesty, and your whole being has been permeated by power and passion for Jesus. So you will go to the ends of the earth if that is what he asks, because you determine to live this life in the light of heaven.

Eternity is calling your soul. It inspires you to awaken, to dream again, and to take risks. It asks you to pursue visions that are shaped not by fear or selfish desires or manipulated emotions, but by the glory of God and the reality of heaven.

ETERNITY IN OUR HEARTS

You were designed to find your home in God, both here during this lifetime and for eternity in heaven. So when you live with heaven set before you, your soul will find satisfaction and health like never before.

I believe the reason many people express a feeling that something isn't right, that something is missing, is because their souls yearn for a closeness with God that cannot be satisfied until they return to the one who created them. As Blaise Pascal, a famous seventeenth-century French mathematician, physicist, inventor, writer, and philosopher, concluded, "This infinite abyss can be filled only with an infinite and immutable object; in other words by God himself."[1]

The great King Solomon put it this way: "[God] has made everything beautiful in its time. He has also set eternity in the human heart" (Ecclesiastes 3:11 NIV). In other words, your soul will never be complete until it finds its eternal home in God. You were made for heaven, and heaven was made for you.

Maybe you need to find yourself by finding God, by seeing life in the light of an eternity that was designed by him and points to him. Your "daily grind," your day-to-day existence, will take on infinite meaning when you realize that the creator of the cosmos is calling you to himself.

Where can your soul find healing and wholeness? Who is the source of ultimate fulfillment? How can you navigate this unpredictable and often painful life?

The answer is God, who reveals his love and grace toward us through Jesus. He is your hope, and he is health for your soul.

Come home to him.

CONCLUSION

Thank you for joining me on this journey! I hope it has helped you become more aware of the needs of your soul. But even more than that, I hope it has encouraged you to let your soul find itself in God; to allow him to love, heal, strengthen, and guide you every day.

The soul-relationship you have with God is unique, beautiful, and completely yours. This book is only the beginning of a lifestyle of knowing him. As you allow his love to fill and flood your soul, you will find a depth of fulfillment you may have never dreamed possible.

Your soul's walk with God is not empty ritual or religion, but a dynamic, organic, and always-new experience with him. You are in a process. You are on a journey. God is at work in your soul, and I truly believe your greatest days are still ahead!

ACKNOWLEDGMENTS

I am so excited to thank the people who made this project possible:

Chelsea

Zion

Eliott

Grace

Mom

Justin

Carla

BJ

Christy

Fetu

Esther

Elijah

Annemarie

Leon

Troy

Teri

Jon

ACKNOWLEDGMENTS

Billy

Mark

And our entire community

And with all my heart JESUS!

NOTES

CHAPTER 2: ORIGINAL HOME

1. Zosia Chustecka, "WHO Clarifies Processed Meat/Cancer Link after 'Bacon Gate,'" Medscape, April 11, 2016, http://www.medscape.com/viewarticle/853566.
2. F. Brown, S. R. Driver, and C. A. Briggs, *Enhanced Brown-Driver-Briggs Hebrew and English Lexicon* (Oxford: Clarendon Press, 1977), 712.
3. "Introduction to Montessori Method," *American Montessori Society*, http://amshq.org/Montessori-Education/Introduction-to-Montessori.

CHAPTER 3: SURPRISED BY MY SOUL

1. Jonah Lehrer, "The Science of Irrationality: Why We Humans Behave So Strangely," *Scientific American*, May 21, 2008, http://www.scientificamerican.com/article/the-science-of-irrational/.

CHAPTER 5: IS LOVE GOD OR IS GOD LOVE?

1. T. Friberg, B. Friberg, and N. F. Miller, *Analytical Lexicon of the Greek New Testament*, vol. 4 (Grand Rapids, MI: Baker Books, 2000), 355.

CHAPTER 6: A QUIET SOUL

1. W. Gesenius, and S. P. Tregelles, *Gesenius' Hebrew and Chaldee Lexicon to the Old Testament Scriptures* (Bellingham, WA: Logos Bible Software, 2003), 809.

CHAPTER 10: HEAVEN

1. Blaise Pascal, *Pensees* (New York: Penguin Books, 1966), 75.

ABOUT THE AUTHOR

Judah Smith is the lead pastor of the City Church in Seattle, Washington. The City Church is a thriving multisite church noted for its cultural relevance, commitment to biblical integrity and faith, and love for Jesus. Judah is known around the United States and the world for his preaching ministry. His fresh, practical, humorous messages demystify the Bible and make Christianity real. Judah is also the author of the *New York Times* bestselling book *Jesus Is _____* and coauthor of *I Will Follow Jesus Bible Storybook*.

ALSO AVAILABLE FROM
JUDAH SMITH

In the rush of living moment to moment, many of us find ourselves simply *surviving*. But if we would take a moment to pause, we'd find the things that matter most in life—*stability, peace, hope, love*—are rooted in the health of what could be called the "inside you." In the *How's Your Soul?* video-based Bible study, author and pastor Judah Smith helps you find your way through the emotional roller coasters of life to discover the soul-healing essentials of *rest, responsibility, restraint*, and *relationships*. This is an invitation to find lasting satisfaction and stability by bringing your feelings into alignment with God's truth, moving beyond surviving to thriving, and learning how to live each day with eternal significance.

"Judah is the most compassionate and giving person I have ever met. His teachings are easy to understand and full of truth and real life."

—Bubba Watson,
Two-time Masters Champion

jesusisbook.com

lifeisbook.tv